THE DERBYSHIRE
YEOMANRY WAR
HISTORY, 1914-1919

LIEUT.-COLONEL G. A. STRUTT, T.D.

*Commanded " A " Squadron on the outbreak of War.
Commanded the Regiment from 1915 until invalided from
Salonica, 1916. At present Commanding the Regiment*

THE DERBYSHIRE YEOMANRY WAR HISTORY

1914–1919

LIEUT.-COLONEL G. A. STRUTT, T.D.

The Naval & Military Press Ltd

❖

Reproduced by kind permission of the Central Library,
Royal Military Academy, Sandhurst

Published by
The Naval & Military Press Ltd
Unit 10, Ridgewood Industrial Park,
Uckfield, East Sussex,
TN22 5QE England
Tel: +44 (0) 1825 749494
Fax: +44 (0) 1825 765701
www.naval-military-press.com
© The Naval & Military Press Ltd 2005

FOREWORD

That the following History of the 1/1st Derbyshire Yeomanry, showing the part which it played in the Great War, leaves much to be desired I am well aware. I wish that the writing of it might have fallen to more able hands than mine, and I hope that readers will pardon my many faults in literary style.

For a part of the time the Regiment was much dispersed, and, in consequence, authentic records were not only hard to keep, but harder to come by. I hope and believe, however, that with the exception of possibly a few minor details as to dates, etc., this History is an accurate account of the life and doings of the Derbyshire Yeomanry between August 8th, 1914, and May 22nd, 1919, on which date the war records of the Regiment close.

G. A. STRUTT (Author),
Lieut.-Colonel.

CONTENTS

CHAPTER XIV

ILLUSTRATIONS

INTRODUCTION

THE 1/1st Derbyshire Yeomanry went to Norfolk August 12th, 1914, and were billeted in villages round Diss and Thrandeston; moved down to Thames Valley end of the month, and were in camp at Moulsford till the beginning of October. Whilst at Moulsford they became part of the 2nd Mounted Division, and, with the South Notts Hussars and the Sherwood Rangers, formed the 3rd Mounted Brigade. At the beginning of October the Regiment moved into billets round Ramsbury, in Wiltshire, where they stayed till the beginning of November, when the whole 2nd Mounted Division were sent to the East Coast, the Regiment being billeted at Cromer and neighbouring villages.

The beginning of April, 1915, all units of the 2nd Mounted Division left the East Coast to embark for overseas. The Regiment left Avonmouth April 13th, arrived Alexandria towards end of the month, encamped first at Sidi Bishr, then moved to Cairo. At the beginning of July, 1915 (whilst the remainder of the Regiment looked after the horses in Cairo), about three-quarters of the Regiment were sent to the Suez Canal, then on August 13th, together with similar detachments from other units of the 2nd Mounted Division, to Gallipoli. They landed at Suvla Bay on August 17th, on the afternoon of the 21st they took part in the big attack. The whole of the 2nd Mounted Division on the Peninsula marched across the Salt Lake, and came under very heavy shell fire, till they reached Chocolate Hill. From there the Notts and Derby Brigade went on to attack the Turkish trenches after dark, and came under heavy rifle fire and machine-gun fire, and owing to the darkness and lack of numbers were unable to get on. During the march across Salt Lake, and in the attack, the

Regiment suffered severe casualties, and were withdrawn to Sala Baba on the night of the 22nd ; from this time up to the date they left the Peninsula, they dug and occupied various trenches on the west of Chocolate Hill. No further attacks were made by either side, but the trenches, through lack of material and the nature of the ground, could not be made safe from shell fire, and sickness, mainly dysentery and jaundice, took a heavy toll of the Regiment. The 2nd Mounted Division remained on Gallipoli till the end of October, when they were moved back to Mudros, thence to Egypt.

The 2nd Mounted Division was now broken up, but the Notts and Derby Brigade went to Mena to reorganize as a mounted brigade. The part of the Regiment which had stayed in Cairo in August had, in the meantime, received reinforcements, and been split up considerably, some had gone to form part of a composite regiment sent out to Salonica, October 15th, others had gone to make up a composite regiment sent with the expedition against the Senussi. By the beginning of February, 1916, the part of the Regiment at Mena had re-equipped and reorganized, and collected most of the men who had been up against the Senussi, and were sent off to Salonica, where they collected the squadron which was already out there, thus becoming a complete mounted regiment again.

The Regiment still remained part of the Notts and Derbyshire Mounted Brigade ; and the South Notts Hussars and the Sherwood Rangers, having reorganized in a similar manner, had also arrived in Macedonia. The Regiment continued as part of the Salonica Expeditionary Force till the end of the war.

From April, 1916, they were employed with the other units of the Brigade patrolling on the Gola Ridge and in the Struma Valley. In the summer of 1916, reduced to a strength of 250 through malaria, the Regiment, under Colonel Neilson, took part in the fighting in the Struma Valley when the Greeks retired from Rupel Pass, and the Bulgars came down into the plain. A

number of casualties occurred on August 20th, until
which day, the Regiment, except for small patrol
actions, had had no serious engagement with the Bulgars.
In the following months the Regiment took part in
various raids against the Bulgars, being, at this period,
part of the 16th Corps, with which corps they remained
for the rest of the war.

When the Brigade was broken up in the Spring of
1917, the Derbyshire Yeomanry remained, and were
kept in the Struma Valley doing patrol work con-
tinuously till the summer of 1918. From October, 1916,
when the Bulgars were driven back from the plain,
the latter occupied the foothills to the north of the
Struma Valley, and the British (later on assisted by
Hellenic troops) occupied those on the southern side.

The Struma Valley, on the left bank of the Struma,
was debatable ground, sometimes a few villages in it
were occupied by Bulgars, sometimes by British or
Greeks ; it was the duty of the Derbyshire Yeomanry
to patrol some part of this valley by day, to observe any
new move on the part of the Bulgars, and to deny
to them villages which were too near our front line.
When the enemy were found to be occupying villages
in the plain, raids on them were often organized, either
by day or night, in which the Regiment took a part.
Patrolling had been the chief duty of the Regiment
since it had been in the country, and some of it was
very arduous work, and especially in the summers of
1916 and 1917 ; the long hours and hot sun tried the
men severely, hardly a single man escaped being down
with malaria—most of them got frequent relapses. In
the summer of 1917, a number of casualties, chiefly
from rifle fire, were sustained ; the country patrolled
was very much overgrown, and our patrols got shot
at most days by the enemy, who were dismounted and
concealed in the undergrowth.

In July, 1918, the Regiment was moved back into
Army Reserve, but was moved forward again two
months later, and taking part in the general advance

on September 23rd, went through the Bulgarian front line some miles to the west of Doiran. They acted as advance guard to the 16th Corps, keeping in touch with the retreating Bulgarian army for about eight days, when hostilities ceased on the arrival of the Bulgarian representatives to negotiate the armistice. The Derbyshire Yeomanry were the first British troops to enter Bulgaria.

COMPLIMENTARY LETTERS, &c.

Extracts from Regimental Orders :

21/7/18.—Copy of a letter from 16th Corps to O.C., 1/1st Derbyshire Yeomanry.

" On the departure of the Derbyshire Yeomanry from the 16th Corps, General Briggs wishes to thank Lieut.-Colonel Neilson, D.S.O., and Officers, N.C.O.'s, and men for the excellent work they have done for him during the period they have served under his command. The zeal, fighting spirit, and sound patrol methods have always evoked his pleasure and admiration. He wishes them every possible good luck, and hopes that if ever an advance takes place on this front that they may again come under his command.

" (*Signed*) E. D. YOUNG,
" Brigadier-General

" July 19th, 1918.   " D.A. & Q.M.G."

See also Regimental Orders or War Diary :

1/10/18.—Letter from 14th Hellenic Division.
2/10/18.—Regimental Order.—C.O.'s appreciation of work done.
11/10/18.—Special order for the day by General Milne.
15/10/18.—Message from His Majesty the King.
5/11/18.—Message from Lieut.-Colonel Neilson on handing over command of Regiment.
25/3/19.—Message from Lieut.-Colonel Tremayne on relinquishing command of Regiment.

LIEUT.-COLONEL LORD HENRY CAVENDISH BENTINCK, T.D.

*Commanded the Regiment from 1913 until invalided from
Gallipoli in 1915*

The Derbyshire Yeomanry War History, 1914-1919

CHAPTER I

MOBILISATION !

I DO not suppose that any member of the Derbyshire Yeomanry in 1914 will forget the receipt of a telegram on August 4th of that year containing the one word " Mobilise " ; still less will he forget the sensations which it aroused, or the feeling of going to school for the first time which probably came over him.

In so far as was possible in a Territorial unit, which had never had any practice in mobilisation in peace time, everything had been carefully worked out before hostilities actually commenced. Telegrams had been addressed to every member of the unit. These were kept filed and ready for instant issue.

Every officer possessed a small book of mobilisation orders, detailing his duties for every day from the time when he joined his Squadron Headquarters, on the first day of mobilisation, until the ninth day, on which the four squadrons were due to assemble in Derby. An officer in each squadron had been detailed to purchase the necessary transport, whilst others were responsible for the collection of horses which had been previously ear-marked by the officer in charge of remounts for the county.

On the outbreak of war the Squadron Headquarters were disposed as follows :—" A " Squadron, Chesterfield ; " B " Squadron, Bakewell ; " C " and " D " Squadrons, and Regimental Headquarters, Derby.

Every squadron store had been well arranged for the rapid issue of equipment, and though short of a considerable amount of clothing, etc., this was forthcoming before the date of the regimental assembly. It must not be supposed from the above that everything was cut and dried, and that the machine ran without a hitch. Far from it. Men turned up promptly, though a number were unavoidably late. This upset the issue of equipment.

Clothing was one of our chief worries. It really appeared at one time as if we possessed no men in the regiment who fitted Government clothing. " Slacks " too long here, sleeves too short there. Here a waist which would not contract sufficiently ; there a tunic, which, though satisfactory in length, would nevertheless contain at least two chests of the size of its owner.

PIT PONIES FOR MOUNTS

But these were by no means our greatest difficulties. It soon became apparent that many of the horses detailed for our use had died, or had been sold, whilst others were totally unsuitable. In the case of " A " Squadron, many of those on the list were pit ponies. About forty of these did not materialise until the day previous to the regiment's assembly at Derby. Many of these ponies, excellent as they were, had not seen the light of day for months, possibly years, and were half blind on reaching daylight. Few had been ridden. As horses dribbled in they had to be allotted to their future owners and their saddlery fitted—an even worse job than fitting the men with clothing.

Then, again, forage had to be collected in more or less unknown quantities as it was required. Delivery was difficult, as the A.S.C. were in process of mobilisation themselves, and in most cases squadron transport was still being collected.

Billeting for man and beast was another difficulty, no one having had any previous experience in the system. Men and horses were in consequence very scattered, and hard to get at when wanted. No officer had had any experience of paying for the same, nor in keeping squadron accounts and pay sheets.

Army Forms innumerable began to pour in, all apparently requiring immediate completion. Every man had to receive a £5 bonus. This part of the mobilisation scheme went quickly and smoothly, until it was discovered that some recipients had subsequently been passed as medically unfit !

As men and horses were equipped they were literally hurled into some sort of training. As the majority of the horses had never had any, and as a number of men were recruits, and therefore in much the same plight, this preliminary training was varied, to say the least of it, and was certainly not without its excitements.

Transport appeared. It varied from a brewer's dray to a milk float.

I fancy that everyone was thankful when the day for assembly at Derby arrived. Tempers were beginning to wear thin, no one knew his head from his heels, or could think of much else than Army Forms and boots.

THE MARCH TO DERBY

The march to Derby proved uneventful in all cases, though no squadron-leader, anxious for the appearance of his men, had cause to bless the enthusiasm of the crowds in their send-off. This was accentuated, in the case of " A " Squadron, by the steep cobbled streets of Chesterfield, and by half-blind and totally untrained pit ponies.

I wonder whether that cinema operator who filmed the march was a humorist !

Derby seemed crowded to its fullest capacity. Billets for the men were hard to find, and stabling for the horses harder still, but all were eventually housed and made more or less comfortable. At all events, every squadron was able to report " All complete " by the time laid down in Mobilisation Orders, and I imagine that everyone heaved a sigh of relief when they realised that mobilisation and all the good-byes were over, and that henceforth the Regiment was to be their home.

Before I conclude this chapter I must refer to what must have been a great blow to " C " Squadron. In order to conform to War Establishment the Regiment had to be reduced from four to three squadrons, and as " C " Squadron happened to be junior squadron at the time it was decided to absorb it into the others. This was accordingly done before we moved from Derby. As there had always been great *esprit de corps* and much friendly rivalry, as was right, between the squadrons, this break-up was very keenly felt, both by officers and men.

Needless to say, the situation was accepted in the best possible spirit after the first disappointment, and though a feeling of regret may have lingered for a time amongst " C " Squadron, every officer and man acted most loyally under the new situation, and " A," " B " and " D " Squadrons benefited proportionately.

CHAPTER II

Home Service

ORDERS were received to entrain the following day, August 12th, and speculation became rife as to our destination. Some, I know, expected to be despatched straight oversea to France, whilst the " German Invasion specialists " put their money on Norfolk, and won. On the 13th the Regiment detrained at Diss, and were billeted in neighbouring villages, chiefly in Thrandaston and Stuston. Here it was a case of every man for himself, as accommodation was very limited and scattered. Fortunately, being early autumn, the horses could all be picketed out.

It was here, chiefly on Stuston Common, that our training commenced in earnest, and with it commenced a stream of inspecting officers, which continued to flow for several months.

The Derbyshire Yeomanry formed part of the Notts and Derby Mounted Brigade, the other two Regiments being the South Notts Hussars and the Sherwood Rangers, who had arrived in the Diss neighbourhood about the same date.

The Brigade was commanded by Brig.-General P. Kenna, V.C., late of the 21st Lancers, and an excellent go-ahead and sound soldier he proved to be. I think at this early stage of the war most of the officers and men in the Regiment, excluding recruits, considered that the Regiment was ready to take the field forthwith. It was as well that we had to do nothing of the sort, as it took a comparatively short time to find how much there was to learn, and how very little we knew.

One of the chief difficulties lay in the fact that no one could possibly form any opinion as to the time likely to be at our disposal for training purposes, nor

could they tell what our rôle was likely to be.   Lieut.-
Colonel Lord Henry Bentinck, who commanded the
Regiment, with his usual sound judgment, left squadron-
leaders a pretty free hand, so long as they confined
themselves to work which would be required in any
eventuality. This was greatly appreciated, as was the
help and advice which he and the Adjutant, Captain
R. H. Brocklebank, 9th Lancers, were always ready to
give.

At this time the first rumours of a projected invasion
reached us, and on more than one occasion the Brigade
was ordered to " stand to " for eventualities.

STREAM OF PAMPHLETS

About now also another apparently inexhaustible
stream commenced. This time from officers serving in
France, who wrote letters and pamphlets, making it
perfectly clear as to just how the thing ought to be
done. Much of this information was most useful, or
might have been so, in tactical work, had a state of
open warfare continued. In any case, it was all
assimilated greedily and put into practice.

As each fresh idea was thoroughly grasped a fresh
theory would be sprung upon us, until we began to
consider ourselves perfect mines of knowledge, and
absolutely " IT."

This epidemic, if I may call it such, was shortly
followed by another, which made its appearance almost
simultaneously with the commencement of trench
warfare.   Trenches, traverses, parapets, and parados
in innumerable variety, and of continually changing
dimensions, now entered our horizon. These kept us
fully occupied, together with mounted work, until we
eventually left England.

It must not be thought that all this took place whilst
we were round Diss. I am merely mentioning it now
to indicate to readers what a tremendous lot had to
be learnt after mobilisation, and how little could really
be expected from any Territorial mounted unit, however

good, when trained in peace time for fifteen days only in the year.

It must not be supposed that tactical training of this sort was the only thing to learn. The internal economy of a troop, a squadron, or of a regiment had to be grappled with. This entailed pay sheets, quittance rolls, messing and squadron accounts, billeting books, etc., etc. In addition, officers had to endeavour to master the " Form of Procedure " of Courts Martial, senior ones by being members of the same, and juniors by attending as " learners."

I should add that physical culture played an important part in the home training, and that at 6.30 a.m. every member of the Regiment might be seen contorting himself into strained positions, varied by sharp sprints, with interludes of " knees up." This portion of the training had a most marked effect, and the rapid development of many of the men was most noticeable.

As time lengthened, it became apparent, in spite of many appeals, that our time was not yet, and instead of the more or less "happy-go-lucky" system of training, to which I originally referred, a definite scheme was adopted throughout the whole Division. This commenced from the rudimentary teachings, and worked up successively to Troop, Squadron, Regimental, Brigade and Divisional Drill. This having been mastered, tactical work and manœuvres were gradually worked up to, and through, the same formations.

" A DRESSING DOWN "

During all this time discipline was being gradually inculcated and strengthened. This was no easy matter in any Territorial unit, where in civil life the individual was usually his own master. Periodically, and just as we were beginning to consider ourselves on a par with the Guards, we would receive a very healthful dressing down on the subject of our laxity. This was never well received, but nevertheless invariably bore good fruit.

For the information of the uninitiated, I may state that the War Establishment of a Yeomanry Regiment was three squadrons of approximately 147 officers and men per squadron.   In addition, there were the Machine-Gun Section, Signallers, and Transport, the personnel of which were drawn from the squadrons.

The permanent staff attached to every regiment consisted of an Adjutant, Quartermaster, Regimental Sergeant-Major, and three Squadron Sergeant-Majors. The help which the Regiment derived from this permanent staff was incalculable.   Whether they raged or were as mild as mother's milk, they were always teaching something.   It was mainly owing to their example and tuition that the Yeomanry non-commissioned officers eventually learnt to " stand on their own legs " and to be self-reliant, a by no means easy virtue to acquire in a Territorial unit, where all are friends, and mostly equals, at home.

As regards the men, the material was excellent, with few exceptions.   As near as I can estimate, some 45 per cent. were farmers or farm labourers, 25 per cent. colliers, mostly from Chesterfield area, and the remainder clerks and tradesmen.   The great majority were men of some means, and possessed a feeling of responsibility.

I always thought that the married men were the most to be relied on, but possibly this was because they may have been older.   On the other hand, it is possible that they may have gone through a period of strict discipline at home !

THE SERGEANT-MAJOR'S " BULL "

About the end of August orders were received for the Brigade to proceed to Moulsford, in the Thames valley.   The Regiment detrained at Reading, and spent the night, a very wet one, there.

It was here that a certain Yeomanry sergeant-major perpetrated the first of many " bulls " attributed to him, by asking the station-master : " Which is the entrance out ? "   On the next day but one the Regiment marched to Moulsford, and went into bivouac on some stubble fields. Fortunately, the weather was glorious.

A lot of useful and very instructive training was carried out during the next fortnight, and the Brigade worked together as a whole for the first time since mobilisation.

It was at this time that the rumour of the Russian Army coming through England first started. As we saw train after train with white-washed windows passing below our camp, we one and all concluded that every train was choc-a-bloc with our allies.

After a fortnight the Brigade was moved across the Thames, so as to be near Churn, where the rest of the regiments which were to form the 2nd Mounted Division, under Major-General Peyton, D.S.O., C.M.G., had assembled. The Notts & Derby Brigade now became the 3rd Mounted Brigade.

During our stay here there was nothing out of the ordinary routine to chronicle, except that our training was extended to Divisional schemes and drill. Some most instructive days we had, too, and some heroic combats, on the great stretch of downs round Churn. It was on these downs that His Majesty King George V. inspected the Division, during the third week in September. A fine sight the Division was, drawn up in line.

Many officers and men had just been inoculated against enteric, and were feeling none too happy in consequence, but I fancy that those who missed this parade were very few.

Immediately after this the whole Regiment received a blow.

A fresh medical inspection was ordered, with the result that we lost the services and companionship of several of our most popular officers. These included Major F. W. Peacock, Second-in-Command of the Regiment, who, during his long connection with it, had made himself almost indispensable. Others who could ill be spared, and whom it would be most difficult to replace, were Major W. D. Winterbottom, commanding " D "

Squadron, and Major F. Gretton, commanding " B " Squadron.

I am sure that they could not have felt the parting more than the Regiment did. For the same cause we lost the services of several excellent N.C.O.'s and some good men.

WINTER BILLETS

We now heard, for the first time, that a second line regiment was to be formed, the formation and command of which was undertaken by Major Winterbottom ; Major Peacock going eventually to the Regimental Headquarters at Derby, to take charge of the adminis-trative centre.

At this time also all ranks were asked to sign on for overseas service, and I regret to say that we thus found ourselves further depleted, though to no serious extent.

As October had come round, and as the cold weather might soon be expected, it was decided to move the Division into billets for the winter. The Derbyshire Yeomanry accordingly marched into Wiltshire at the beginning of the month. Here they found excellent billets and much hospitality, Headquarters, with " B " and " D " Squadrons, being billeted round Ramsbury, and " A " Squadron at Aldbourne.

Whilst here much of our time was devoted to musketry on extemporised ranges, and as this was the first opportunity we had had to instruct our recruits in the use of their arms, or to improve the shooting of the remainder, full use was made of our time and a most marked improvement was shown.

To a limited extent we were able to carry out field practices ; often, I fear, to the annoyance of the numerous trainers, who had their quarters round about. Although it must have been a frequent cause for annoyance, and though many gallops must have been interfered with, I never heard a single word of com-plaint.

About now we were issued with swords, which opened up still another field of training for us.

Occasionally, Lord Henry Bentinck would indulge the Regiment in " shock tactics," and the wild gallops which ensued were enjoyed by everyone. Had the charges been made in reality I fear that our gallant Colonel would have lost his life on each and every occasion, long before the Regiment could have rendered any assistance.

THE CORPORAL'S LAPSE

On these occasions wise squadron-leaders detailed a party to follow in the wake of the Regiment, to pick up shed gear. By this means I more than once made good all previous deficiencies !

It was here, I remember, a general favourite of the Regiment, who had long served in the ranks, was at long last promoted to corporal. It was here, too, one week later, my sad duty to order the removal of the coveted stripes.

Corporal C—— had, alas, gazed on the wine when it was at its reddest.

On being asked his explanation, he spake in this wise :

" Well, Sir, it's these 'ere stripes as dun it. I 'ad to drink their 'ealths, so I wet 'em an' then I must a wet 'em again, and now seemingly I've washed 'em out."

Meanwhile things had been going none too well in France, so that we were not altogether surprised when we got more or less sudden orders to move to a place " Destination unknown."

It was rumoured that Cromer was our objective, and in consequence some consternation was felt by " A " Squadron when they found themselves on Parkstone Quay, Harwich, at 11 p.m. one bitterly cold night. Surprising to say, they were greeted with the greatest enthusiasm. I regret to say that this was somewhat modified when their identity was made known, and they were revealed for their true worth, and not as a long-expected battery of artillery due for overseas.

After consuming the food prepared for a draft expected from India, the Squadron again set forth, and this time arrived at their right destination, which proved to be Cromer, as prognosticated.

Cromer was reached at 2 a.m., and the remainder of the Regiment was located, bivouacked in a turnip field. It was a bitterly cold night, but everyone was sufficiently tired not to mind that, or even the loose horses, which periodically jumped fences in the dark, invariably landing close to one's head. So everyone said.

With daylight, it transpired that a raid was expected, and just as we were preparing to move to our respective destinations the raid appears to have been cancelled. We were accordingly switched off elsewhere, and eventually arrived in the neighbourhood of Barningham, some eight miles from the coast. Here we met with the usual hospitality.

Three weeks were spent in this neighbourhood, during which time there were several alarms, usually during the darkest part of a darkest night. On these occasions it was " boot and saddle " in the dark, followed by a march in inky blackness to the regimental rendezvous, a march to the coast, followed by a weary return with daylight.

A good deal was learnt about regimental and squadron transport on these occasions.

THE EAST COAST

Towards the close of November the Brigade was moved down to the coast itself, it being felt that its previous position was too distant from the threatened spots should the worst happen. Cromer became the Headquarters of the Regiment, together with " B " and " D " Squadrons, whilst " A " Squadron was divided between East and West Runton, respectively two and three miles north of Cromer. The remainder of the Brigade were billeted in and around Sheringham.

Our first task was to entrench the four miles of coast in our area. This was carried out to the best of our ability, though, I fear, the resultant trenches would have served no purpose whatever had a raid been made. This was chiefly owing to an almost entire lack of wire and timber.

Our stay in the Cromer area lengthened out to the beginning of April, 1915, during which time much useful work was done. Discipline was tightened up, recruits and drafts were trained, many bad and unsuitable horses were got rid of, and a very fair class of remount drawn in their place.

Squadron and regimental drills, etc., were of almost daily occurrence, each squadron now being required to furnish a scheme of training for the ensuing week. We were most fortunate in having Cromer Park and Felbrigg Park within easy distance, and it was in these that most of the work was done.

In addition to the ordinary routine of training, other and far less pleasant duties fell to our lot. Squadrons took it in turns to guard the coast a little north of Weybourne. This meant that a squadron had to leave its billets at about 2 a.m., march nine miles on tarred roads, frequently covered by a skim of ice, so as to arrive on the beach two hours before sunrise. Here it had to wait until one hour after sunrise, when it was at liberty to return home.

ALARMS AND SEARCH FOR SPIES

There were few incidents worthy of record whilst at Cromer, though few will forget Christmas Eve. A wire having been received from the Admiralty that German transports had put to sea, the Regiment was ordered to its alarm posts, *i.e.*, our trenches on the edge of the cliffs. In these trenches we spent our night, which happened to be a particularly cold one, with a hard frost, and it was not until 11 a.m. that we received the "All clear" report. Probably no one enjoyed their Christmas dinner any the worse in consequence.

It was during our stay here that the spy mania

really throve. Reports of mysterious lights and signalling at night became so numerous that one was led to ask oneself whether the whole population were not German spies in disguise of loyal Englishmen. One remarkably suspicious case was reported. The suspected house was surrounded and searched, the occupants put to the question, and a thoroughly melodramatic air created. This was on Christmas Day, the morning of our all-night vigil. At last the spy was unearthed—a flapping blind at the end of a passage and a lamp carried by the lady of the house as she went to her baby's room to fill its Christmas stocking!

About now Major F. Lance, Indian Cavalry, was appointed second-in-command to the Regiment.

During March the first Zeppelin raid took place— Sheringham was bombed from a very low altitude, but very little material damage was done.

HUMOROUS SERGEANT-MAJORS

The humorous incidents which I recollect at this time are few. The same sergeant-major of the Reading incident was one day heard to give the order : " Push it away towards yer," an order somewhat difficult to execute.

Once this awful threat was overheard : "If you do that again, I'll make you mark time all the way home!"

On another occasion a recruit, having lost his oats through a hole in his nose-bag, was heard to report to his squadron sergeant-major that he "had lost his seed," and was met with the prompt retort : "What are you riding, a —— canary ?"

During this prolonged stay in England, General Peyton had made continued appeals to the War Office, and to Lord Kitchener in person, that the Division might be sent oversea, even if dismounted, all, however, without avail. I think we had almost resigned ourselves to a stay in England " for the duration," when, towards the end of March, 1915, strong rumours began to circulate that at last we were to go, and in a few days, to everyone's delight, these were confirmed, though no destination, naturally, was given.

Speculation was fairly evenly divided between France, Egypt, India and East Africa. Speculation is always idle, and we had plenty to do making a thorough overhaul of all equipment, drawing fresh clothing and generally fitting out to the last button. This, of course, applied to the whole 2nd Mounted Division.

Definite orders were at last received, and the Regiment, after its last farewells, left Cromer by rail for Avonmouth on April 12th. After the last partings all were comparatively light-hearted, but I doubt if any would have been so had they known then that it would be over four years before the Regiment was to return.

On April 13th the three regiments of the Brigade embarked and sailed on the transport *Saturnia*, the horses going in other ships, under horse-conducting parties drawn from the regiments.

CHAPTER III

EGYPT

THE voyage to Egypt, which we learnt, on reaching Gibraltar, was our destination, was without event, so far as our ship was concerned. A horse transport which sailed two hours before we did, and which contained horses of the Worcestershire and Warwickshire Yeomanries, was torpedoed, and a number of horses lost. Fortunately, this happened off the Scillies and the ship was able to reach Ireland.

It was fortunate that we had beautiful weather and a smooth sea the whole way, as the ship was crammed, and overcrowded as regards the boats and lifebelts, which were quite inadequate in numbers. The days were started with physical drill at an early hour, followed by a general clean-up between decks and an inspection of the whole ship. The afternoons were frequently devoted to boxing competitions.

On the ninth day after leaving England we reached Alexandria, our port of disembarkation, and were shortly followed by our horse boat. These, our kit and transport, were landed, and the Regiment received orders to march to, and bivouac at, Sidi Bish, about twelve miles east of Alexandria itself. Our actual bivouac was in the desert, and right on the seashore.

Everything pointed to a delightful picnic, but we were soon disillusioned on this score, when flies of a most pestilential breed, and apparently in millions, assailed us. Nor were matters improved when we found that the camp had been previously occupied by a regiment of Chasseurs d'Afrique, whose traces had been obliterated by the sand, but which nevertheless soon reappeared on the surface, to the general discomfort of everyone. This was prejudicial to the

LIEUT.-COLONEL W. D. WINTERBOTTOM, T.D.

Served 35 years in the Regiment. Formed 2nd Line Regiment when 1st Line was ordered abroad

health of officers and men, and a number went down
with a variety of low fever.

DISCOMFORTS OF THE CLIMATE

Parties of men were allowed to visit Alexandria.
I met one such party on their return, and, thinking
they were looking pale about the gills, enquired where
they had been, and was told " to the native slaughter-
house." With a temperature of well over 100 degrees
in the shade, it is no wonder that one and all had
succumbed immediately on entering.

After ten days at Sidi Bish the Regiment received
orders to entrain for Cairo, much to everyone's delight,
and this city we reached early in the first week of May.

On arriving there we were most fortunate in finding
that we had been allotted the new Abbas Hilmi barracks
at Abbassia. We were thus within easy reach of Cairo,
but yet on the edge of the desert, so that we had no
tedious marches in the early mornings to get on to
our parade ground, nor had we to toil back to barracks
in the stifling heat after the sun was up.

Now was the period of the "hamseens"—hot scorching
winds from off the desert, accompanied by dense clouds
of fine sand. The worst of these which we experienced
reached a temperature of 120 degrees in the shade.
Out of doors it was unbearable, the roads themselves
being almost too hot to stand on.

Immediately on our arrival covered standings had
been erected for the horses, and these stood the heat,
to which they were quite unused, remarkably well,
and, in fact, actually gained in condition. All drill
and training was carried out in the early mornings,
parade being soon after dawn, and the men were entirely
exempt from work during the afternoons, with the
exception of having to attend evening stables. No
doubt, to this was due our almost complete immunity
from cases of sunstroke.

I wish the same could have been said of an Australian
Brigade camped not far away. These poor fellows

c

were bivouacked under single bell tents ,which offered very little protection from the sun, and many deaths occurred in consequence.

The desert provided us with a magnificent training ground, and full use was made of its possibilities, particularly as regards advance guard, rear guard and patrol work in all its branches. This work in an open country devoid of habitation or landmarks, and of a most confusing character, did a great deal towards developing the initiative of the men.

COMPASS RACES

Compass races at night were occasionally held, with excellent results. The usual procedure on these occasions was as follows : The competitors were started in pairs at intervals of ten minutes. On starting, a pair would be given a certain compass bearing, and to this they had to go at the best speed at which they could get their horses over the rough country. If the direction was successfully maintained, they would find after about two miles, a man with a dark lantern. His duty would be to take their time, and give them a fresh bearing, which would bring them to a second and eventually, if they held the line, to a third, and home.

I remember one race of about five-and-a-half miles being won in the time of thirty minutes. Allowing for the time taken to set one's compass at least thrice, and select one's star on which to march, this was decidedly good travelling at night.

Brigade drill was frequent, and few will forget the dense clouds of sand stirred up, or the extraordinary formations we occasionally found the Brigade in when the halt had been sounded and the dust allowed to subside. The difficulties met with greatly improved both squadron and troop leading, and it was not long before dust clouds appeared to be no handicap.

More ambitious schemes, in which the whole Division were engaged, plus the Westminster Dragoons and

Herts Yeomanry, who were now attached to us, took place under General Peyton's direction. These schemes usually covered two days and one night, and many interesting operations were carried through. These usually meant a difficult night march for two or more Brigades.

At this period we were unfortunate in losing the services of Major W. S. Power, D.S.O., who was invalided home.

This state of things was too good to last, and on July 8th we received orders to move to the Suez Canal. We duly entrained at Abbassia on July 12th, arriving at Suez at 5.30 a.m. on the following morning. Here we went into bivouac alongside the Rough Riders, forming with them the 28th Brigade M.E.F.

A proportion of men and most of the horses were ordered to remain at Cairo, so that the strength of the Regiment at Suez numbered only 410 men and 157 horses, chiefly Machine-Gun Section, Transport and Signals.

Our camp here was a most unattractive spot, being four miles outside Suez, three miles from the sea, and plump in the desert, with not a tree within a mile of us, no shade and myriads of flies.

Guards were found for the Victoria Convalescent Hospital, Canal Locks and Arbain Wireless Station.

DECEIVED BY THE MIRAGE

On our first morning there we were told that we might take the men to bathe. Having noticed the previous evening a most attractive-looking lake, surrounded with palm trees and dotted with beds of rushes, apparently not more than a mile distant, it took me no time to decide on *my* bathing place.

We marched, the whole squadron, many a weary mile, and returned to camp unwashed and unrefreshed. The whole alluring scene had proved to be a mirage.

Sometimes that infernal lake came almost up to the camp, but never reached it.

As there were so few horses with the Regiment, these were used exclusively for riding school, which took place every day.

Here, too, we indulged in mild race meetings, which usually took the form of matches between the fastest or fattest or slowest horses. I don't think much money changed hands on these occasions.

On July 22nd the Regiment was inspected by Lieut.-General F. G. Wilson, V.C., commanding the canal defences. Those who participated will remember the two hours during which we stood in the grilling sun awaiting this officer's arrival. The power of the sun at Suez in mid-July is not to be scoffed at. No doubt, the delay was unavoidable, but we all thought that a word of explanation might have been offered.

At this period the Canal defences were situated on the actual banks of the canal itself, and consisted of a series of posts, or redoubts, a few miles apart.

The Turkish attack had been repulsed in March, and there were now no formed bodies of the enemy in the immediate neighbourhood, though considerable forces were reported some forty miles east of the canal. The chief danger to be feared was from small parties attempting to slip between the different posts, with the intention of depositing mines in the canal.

PATROLLING THE CANAL

It will be readily understood that even one tramp steamer successfully sunk might easily block our route from Australia and India at a most critical time. To counter this danger a system of patrols was constantly maintained along the canal banks, whilst small flying columns were employed to search the desert further afield, with orders to follow up any fresh tracks which they met with in the sand. Aeroplanes at this time would have been invaluable, but we never saw one.

In the last week of July " A " Squadron, under Major G. A. Strutt, were ordered to take over the so-called fort at El Shatt. This was on the east side of the canal, and immediately above its lower entrance. In addition to the Yeomanry, the garrison of El Shatt consisted of a company of the 30th Baluchis, a few Bikanir Camel Corps and a section of Hyderabad Lancers.

This very mixed force went to form a small flying column, a rather weird combination of cavalry and infantry drill being devised to meet the situation.

During our stay here no Turks were met with, only a few wandering Arabs being haled into the post for examination.

This system of defence for the all-vital canal subsequently constrained Lord Kitchener to demand of a certain General in high command whether he was defending the canal or whether the canal was defending him ?

OFF TO GALLIPOLI

On August 10th orders were suddenly received for the Regiment to proceed to Cairo immediately, and by midday we had all entrained and were well on our way, duly reaching our destination the same evening. On our arrival, it became known that the whole of the 2nd Mounted Division, consisting of fourteen Yeomanry Regiments, was to be immediately dismounted and proceed to Gallipoli.

Each regiment, moreover, was ordered to select 350 officers and men, the remainder being left in charge of the horses. These 350 were to be divided into two squadrons or double companies.

This process of selection was a most difficult and unenviable task. Every officer and man was anxious to go, and after weeding out those least physically fit in all three squadrons it was decided, in addition, to leave those officers and men who could be relied on to handle a large number of horses to the best advantage during the absence of the rest of the Regiment.

We were allowed less than twenty-four hours in which to complete the new arrangement. " Nominal rolls " had to be prepared, saddlery handed in to store, and fresh equipment (infantry) drawn and issued. Kit had to be sorted out to the barest necessities. No one knew how to put our new web equipment together. Still, it was put together somehow, and usually managed to remain on its owner's back until we embarked, when we were shown by the sailors how to do it correctly !

It was a feverish and somewhat hectic twenty-four hours, nevertheless it just sufficed, and we found ourselves on board the train for Alexandria the following evening.

Before leaving Cairo, so to speak, I wish to put it on record that although the men had more or less free access into that city, during all the time that the Regiment was at Abbassia, I do not remember a single instance of any man having to be punished for any offence or misconduct whatsoever. I think this is undoubted proof of the high standard of discipline up to which Lord Henry Bentinck had worked the Regiment, and also of the fine material of which it was composed.

CHAPTER IV

GALLIPOLI

WE sailed from Alexandria on the night of August 13th, and after a good run, which was protracted by having to steer a rather circuitous course to avoid submarines, arrived at the harbour of Mudros during the morning of the 17th.

Mudros is a magnificent harbour, capable, we were told, of holding as many as 400 big ships, and it looked delightful to us, sick of Egypt and its sand, to see steeply rising hills covered with grass, burnt yellow it is true, and masses of shipping in the harbour, with— and this appealed to us most—a cool sky overhead.

Every sort of ship was there—warships, both French and British, transports, colliers, tugs, paddle boats from the Clyde, Thames steamers and Irish Packet boats. One or two ships were lying there, too, which had evidently been torpedoed.

In the afternoon an Irish packet boat, the *Partridge*, came alongside, and 800 of us were crowded on board like herrings. As soon as we had got everything aboard, we started for Suvla Bay, which we had learnt by then was our destination.

Just before leaving Alexandria we had heard rumours of a landing having been made at Suvla, but had heard no details, and as this was our first opportunity of gleaning any we naturally bombarded the crew of that boat with questions.

To our disappointment, they informed us that when they had left Suvla two days before they had seen villages burning half way across the peninsula, and that doubtless by now we should only have to walk across it and occupy the ground which had already been captured. We were soon to be disillusioned.

THE FLASH OF THE GUNS

As we steamed along all that night, parallel to the coast, we could constantly see the flashes of heavy guns in the darkness, and hear their rumble faintly. I think a feeling of unreality possessed everyone of us. After being mobilised for a year without having heard a shot fired, it was certainly difficult to realise that at long last we were to take our share in events, and probably all offered up a silent prayer that they would not be found wanting when it came to the real test.

Just before dawn on the 18th we crept into Suvla Bay in the pitch dark. Other boats were ahead of us, and had already started to disembark, as one could tell by the creak of oars on rowlocks. Although we were all ready to do the same, we had to await our turn, and it was not until daylight that it came.

With daylight one could see our surroundings for the first time: a shallow crescent-shaped bay, perhaps two miles in width, with low rocky shores. Rough boulder-strewn ground rose gradually from the shore for a distance of about half a mile, after which it rose more steeply till it reached a crest of some 400 feet in height.

This ridge followed nearly parallel to the shore till it tapered down to the northern promontory of the bay. To the south it turned inland out of our sight, and from the angle so formed a slight spur ran down at right angles, merging into the shore almost opposite our anchorage. Further to the right, or south, the country appeared much more level, in fact, almost dead flat, and this plain receded inland for some two miles before reaching some slight foothills.

The plain we became familiar with under the name of " Salt Lake," and the foothills under that of " Chocolate Hill."

THE FAMOUS ANZAC COVE

Immediately behind this the hills became high, steep and rugged, gradually curving round to the south until they met the coast four miles further down. This point, we afterwards learnt, was the famous Anzac.

The hills thus formed a natural amphitheatre, with the Salt Lake Plain as the arena, and a bloody arena it became. At the apex, so to speak, of this arena two deep valleys converged, separated by a steep wedge-shaped shoulder of hill, now known as Hill 112. Almost immediately at the foot of this lay Chocolate Hill.

Each of these valleys led almost directly across the peninsula, and formed the gateways, the seizure of which had been the object of the landing on August 10th. Each of these valleys contained an important village : that to the north, Anafarta, and that to the south, Biyuk Anafarta. The beds of these valleys were dried water-courses.

To return to the coast. Midway between the Suvla anchorage and Anzac a long narrow promontory projected into the sea. This was Lala Baba, and formed the southern horn of the bay. Lala Baba itself gradually rose from the plain in front until it formed a hump-backed hill, possibly a hundred feet high, terminating in low cliffs above the shore.

Having described the terrain, and before proceeding with the narrative of events, it will be best to give a short summary of what had happened previous to our arrival.

A SURPRISE ATTACK

On August 8th General Stopford's force was landed at Suvla Bay, somewhere, I gathered, near Lala Baba. This force landed at night, and was composed of Regular Divisions and also two of Kitchener's Divisions, who had recently arrived from England, and had never been in action.

Previous to this landing the Australians and New Zealanders had made their famous landing at Anzac Cove, and were holding the southern spur of hills, which I have mentioned, for approximately a mile inland.

As the element of surprise was essential for the success of the landing, a strong bombardment, followed by an attack, was launched on Achi Baba by the force operating from Cape Helles, the southern extremity of the peninsula.

This attack immediately preceded the Suvla landing, and was designed to draw down to Cape Helles the Turkish Reserve Divisions, which were concentrated about the Bulair lines which run across the northern end of Gallipoli.

The attack succeeded so admirably in achieving this object that at the time of the landing only the Turkish rear-guard, consisting of two regiments of gendarmerie, with six guns, were available to support the few troops which were watching the coast. In fact, the element of surprise was certainly with us.

Many reasons have been given for the failure of the attack, but from enquiries from those who had taken part in it, the following seem to have been the chief factors.

REASONS FOR FAILURE

No one seems to have been given definite orders as to the objective, and consequently determined leadership was frequently lacking. Some formations acted with great initiative, and must have reached well inland, certainly as far as Biyuk Anafarta, which was set on fire. These, partly from lack of support and partly from the men having drunk all the water they carried, and as no arrangements appear to have been made for a further supply, had to fall back and dig in where best they could.

Some of the newly-formed Kitchener Brigades appear to have acted with little dash or initiative, probably owing to lack of information, for, going over the ground afterwards, one could see where units had started to dig themselves in within a few hundred yards of the shore, in spite of what must have been slight opposition.

Again, there were many circumstantial stories of

both Ghurkas and New Zealanders having reached the crest of Saribahr, a dominating hill of vital importance, only to be mistaken for enemy and shelled off it by the heavy guns of the fleet.

In extenuation of this it must be borne in mind that though the plain of the Salt Lake was dead flat, it was nevertheless covered with thick scrub, which not only made leadership extremely difficult, unless carried out with full knowledge and great determination, but provided ideal cover for snipers. This form of warfare the Turks not only excelled in, but on this occasion utilised to the best advantage.

For unseasoned troops there can be nothing more disconcerting than to hear rifle fire going on in every direction, and with it no knowledge as to whether it is proceeding from friend or foe. It becomes impossible to know whether your own troops are in front or whether you are cut off. Unless orders had been issued to force the way across *at all costs*, it was only reasonable to expect that the attack must be held up and eventually broken, as was the case here.

By August 10th the attempt to seize the heights had definitely failed, and I imagine that it was then that the 2nd Mounted Division were wired for.

At the time of our arrival the position must have been practically the same as it was left after the close of the attack on the 10th. On the right flank the position at Anzac was the same in depth as it was before the attack, though their left flank had been extended for nearly a mile across the plain. This extension of line was, I believe, held by an Irish Brigade and a battalion of Ghurkas.

On the northern side of the plain our line ran from a point just short of, and rather to the north of Chocolate Hill, stretching almost due north till it reached the crest of Karakol, the ridge to which I referred as being immediately above Suvla Bay. There was thus a considerable gap between the two forces.

At the time of our landing General Stopford had been recalled, and Major-General De Lisle had taken over command pending the arrival of General Byng.

WE LAND

After this digression let us return to where we left the Regiment on board the *Partridge*, but before proceeding further it must be understood that, as yet, we knew nothing of the situation as it really was, and fully believed that the crossing of the peninsula had been virtually effected.

With the first signs of daylight this delusion was quickly dispelled. Almost the first thing which we saw was a flash, followed by a bang, which we fondly put down to one of our own guns firing, as we had been told that the enemy could no longer reach the beach. When a few minutes later the same phenomena recurred, and we saw people run to the spot and carry something away, we began to class our informant as a liar.

A few minutes later we were ordered into the boats and rowed to the shore, which was only a few hundred yards distant. Here we landed at " K " beach, a small temporary landing-slip, which was already crowded with men of other regiments awaiting the boats with their kit and ammunition.

We soon realised that we must be in full view of the Turk as shells began to arrive fairly freely. These were mostly H.E. (high explosive) fifteen-pounders, and did practically no damage, although the shooting was fairly accurate. It was by no means a pleasant reception; however, I know that the sensations of all the officers were mingled with a good deal of elation and satisfaction when they saw how the men stood their baptism of fire.

A letter which I have before me reads : " A good deal of delay was caused in unlading the boats, as, whenever a shell was heard approaching, the men would drop whatever they were carrying, not from funk, but in order to obtain a better view of the burst."

The attention of the Turks was not confined to the pier only, for they every now and again switched on to some boat as it rowed ashore, and particularly good practice they made at one containing Major Lance, wetting the occupants through with two consecutive shells.

The day was very hot, and it was no mean job carrying all our impedimenta by hand from the slip to a flat, stony piece of ground half a mile away, which had been allotted to the Division as a bivouac.

THE " MIDDAY HATE "

After being moved two or three times, we eventually appeared to have reached our own allotment, and were told to dig in, as shells were still coming along.   Beyond removing a few inches of surface soil, this proved to be an impossibility, as the ground was solid rock. However, on these occasions even two or three stones up-ended prove to be a great moral comfort.

A scrappy breakfast was prepared, and I well remember, as an appetiser, some well-intentioned stretcher-bearers carried a dead man, minus one arm, through our midst just as we were preparing to consume it.

We had all comfortably settled down, when fresh orders were issued for the Division to move immediately to fresh ground further up the hill, which I have already mentioned as running parallel to the shore, as the ground on which we had settled like a swarm of locusts was a favourite practice-ground for the Turks at their " midday hate," due in half an hour.

In half an hour the ground was clear !

Our new position was a great improvement.   Here the ground was less rocky, and shelter trenches of sorts could be, and were, made.   We also had a certain amount of cover from view afforded by the spur of hill which ran down to the shore.   Above all, we were well above the bay and could look down on the lower ground, noting with interest the bursting of the shells, which were arriving at the rate of about one a minute. It was most interesting to see men, evidently new arrivals, like ourselves, running to where a shell had burst to pick up the bits as mementoes. I expect this phase soon passed.

Everyone was about tired out that night, but we were to get little sleep. About 9 p.m. rifle fire broke out behind the ridge on which we were, and this soon became intense. So furious was it that one felt it must cease after a few minutes, as there could be nothing left alive on either side; nevertheless, it continued with unabated vigour till daylight.

A HEAVY BOMBARDMENT

Soon after daylight (this was the 19th), the guns of the Fleet, which was lying off Lala Baba, commenced a steady fire, which increased to a heavy bombardment towards midday.

Realising that " something was on," those who could get away went to the top of the ridge to see what could be seen.

And a wonderful sight it was as we looked on to the plain below. The Fleet appeared to be shelling Chocolate Hill and the ground to its right or south. Across the plain itself could be seen lines of men advancing in extended order, where the scrub permitted, or converging and forming into short columns when progress through the scrub became difficult.

Every small body of troops was being systematically followed up, or searched for, by the enemy's shrapnel and H.E. Occasionally, one could see a shell burst in the middle of a group, but without doing much apparent harm.

The troops seemed to have started somewhere from in front of Lala Baba, and to be converging on Chocolate Hill and to its immediate left; whilst other bodies, though they were difficult to make out, were moving midway across the plain to its right.

A constant thin stream of men could be seen making their way slowly back to the beach, where the Red Cross tents could be descried.

Towards 3 p.m. the firing died down and eventually
ceased.

This operation was successful, and succeeded in
making Chocolate Hill good, and also in linking it up
with the troops to the right, *i.e.*, with those holding
Anzac and the plain immediately to its left, or north.

It was not until this gap had been filled that further
operations were possible.

NIGHTLY RIFLE FIRE

During the night which followed there was further
heavy rifle fire, this time from the hills at Anzac. So
intense was it at times that the lines of whole trenches
could be followed from the almost continuous flash of
the rifles.

During all the time that we were on the peninsula
the absence of rifle fire by day and its never-ending
crackle by night was most noticeable. The latter
mostly came from the Turks, who required, it seemed,
the least provocation to set them off. Their fire,
though rapid and continuous, was always wild.

Conversely, their guns, which fired fairly steadily
by day, never spoke at all at night, except on very
rare occasions. This was doubtless owing to their
positions on the hills, and their consequent fear of
betraying them by the flash. Excellent gun positions
they must have had, too, owing to the hillsides being
creased with innumerable folds and ridges, making
observation almost impossible.

VISIT OF GERMAN TAUBES

August 20th proved to be a day of speculation and
preparation, for during the morning we were told that
the Division was to go into action the following day.
Of speculation there was much, and that remained
unsatisfied. Of preparation there was little, as there
was nothing to prepare. It was decided that 300 men
from each regiment were to participate, and that the
seconds-in-command of each of the two squadrons, or
companies, were to be left at our bivouac, and with

each a subaltern. Little weeding out was required to pick the 300, as this was all we could muster, after providing for guards, etc., over the kit.

All officers in the Division were to attend a lecture on bombs down on the beach. The lecturer, mounted on two or three recently landed cases of bombs, expatiated on their mechanism and use. It was exceedingly interesting, as no one had previously seen a bomb. It was also exceedingly dangerous, we thought, as everyone felt that we were presenting the chance of a lifetime to the Turk. But, probably, the midday hate was hardly due. After the lecture was over we felt that the enemy had deliberately put a slight upon us by thus ignoring so valuable a target.

Be that as it may, not a single bomb was issued to any regiment, which was probably just as well. It was, indeed, at least ten days before a small issue was made, and then those proved to be of an entirely different pattern—not that that really mattered.

During the afternoon two German Taubes flew over, apparently with the intention of bombing the fleet, but after a few rounds of A.A. (anti-aircraft) they disappeared whence they came. These were the first enemy aeroplanes we had seen.

The afternoon was spent in writing letters and in watching the enemy shell the mules as they went to water. These animals were small Indian mules under native drivers, and they appeared to take singularly little interest in the proceedings, even when shells fell right amongst them. Little damage was done as a rule, though it was reported that on one occasion no less than ninety-five were killed or wounded by one shrapnel burst.

Whilst mentioning the subject of water it should be remembered that this necessity, or rather the lack of it, was one of our greatest difficulties.

No wells existed near the beach, and the ground was too rocky to sink any, nor were there any streams. Every drop of water, therefore, both for man and beast,

MAJOR F. W. PEACOCK, T.D., C.M.G.

Second in Command of the Regiment on the outbreak of War. Served 35 years in the Regiment. Took over Administrative Centre 1st Line Regiment at Derby when the Regiment proceeded overseas   Chairman of the Territorial Army Association

had to be brought ashore from ships. This not only meant great labour, but great scarcity also, and all ranks were in consequence limited to one quart a day.

On more than one occasion the Turks—or, rather, the Germans, for the enemy's guns were almost entirely manned by the latter—hit the water tanks as they were coming ashore, and then matters became really serious. At the best of times the water was both dirty and bad.

CHAPTER V

GALLIPOLI—*continued*

TOWARDS evening we were told that the Division was to march as soon as it became dark to Lala Baba, where we were to spend the night before the battle. All machine-guns in the Division were to move direct to Chocolate Hill, where they were to be massed and used to cover the infantry attack on the following day.

Each regiment possessed two Maxim guns, ours being under the command of Captain J. Sherrard. Every man was ordered to carry 150 rounds of ammunition, as well as either a pick or a shovel.

A CURIOUS INCIDENT

At 6 p.m. the Division formed up in mass, in a dip behind the spur which I have mentioned, preparatory to moving off. Just before we moved a shell dropped almost in our midst. Although it did not burst, everyone was astonished to see what resembled a rocket soar up from it as it landed. Doubtless, there was no significance in it, but it served to convey the impression that the enemy knew just where we were, and all about us.

The march to Lala Baba was exceedingly hot and wearisome, well laden as all were, for though the distance was not more than two miles, this was through the soft, heavy sand above the shore. Each regiment as it reached Lala Baba was halted, and ordered to lie down where it was for the night, and a very cold night it was.

Before daybreak next morning the Division was moved to the cover of the low cliffs on the beach. Here we were out of sight, and could light our fires for breakfast.

Orders were issued for the Division to parade at midday, and we were informed that our rôle was to act as support to the infantry, who were to deliver an attack, also that the Division was to be commanded by General Kenna during the operation, and that General Peyton was to command the Corps. Beyond this, neither officers nor men were given any information whatsoever. A dead secrecy, which was fatal to success, was maintained by those in high command. Doubtless, the intention of preventing the enemy from gleaning any information was excellent, especially as spies were known to be numerous behind our lines. It is not my intention to criticise, but merely to point out facts as we found them.

Of course, it took little intelligence to decide that Hill 112 must of necessity be a chief objective, but whether that was the only one, or whether a break right across was contemplated, was a matter of speculation. We were entirely ignorant both as to the part we were intended to play and also as to even the outline of the infantry's plan of attack. No one possessed a map or had even seen one. Apparently, all the teaching of the text-books as to the importance of the fullest possible information, and of the necessity for every individual knowing what was expected of him—a teaching which had been insisted on ever since training started—had gone by the board.

OBJECT OF THE ATTACK

As things turned out, it was not until two months later, when someone got a copy of *The Times*, that we, the participants, learnt what we had been trying to do. I cannot guarantee that this report is correct, but I think it is substantially so. It read as follows :—

The first attempt to seize the hills round Anafarta having definitely broken down by the morning of August 10th, it required time to sort and reorganise the units, to collect the wounded, and to land stores, ammunition, and artillery before any fresh attempt could be made against the position, and it was not until August 21st that the army was in a position to make a frontal attack on the Turks in this quarter. The prizes which would be the reward of success were great, and fully justified a supreme effort. This ten days' interval was, of course, made full use of by the enemy, who, now knowing definitely where our main blow would fall, was able to release his divisions in the north, stationed round Bulair, and bring some of them to the threatened point.

All hope of effecting a surprise had now vanished, and it was obvious that the position comprised within the sector stretching from Hill 70 to Hill 112, the line chosen for our assault, could only be taken by a frontal attack and sheer hard fighting. Meanwhile, the Turks had made full use of the time afforded them, and, according to their invariable practice, had dug themselves in up to their necks. Every dawn disclosed new trenches which had been dug in the night, and it was obvious from the manner in which they searched our beaches and camps with shell fire that several fresh batteries had been brought to this front.

Opposite our trenches, in the open, the Turks had also dug two lines, of immense strength and carefully loopholed. Our immediate objective on the left was the capture of Hill 70, according to the map, or Burnt Hill among the troops, which lies in front of the main position, and which had caused us so much trouble ever since the landing.

Our centre and right were to advance from the ridge in front of Chocolate Hill, or Yilghin Burnu, as it is marked on the map, and from the trenches in the plain south of it, and, after capturing the Turkish trenches in the low ground in their immediate front, were to converge and assault the main objective, Hill 112.

For this supreme effort troops were massed along the line Hill 70 to Hill 112, and a Division of Yeomanry, without their horses, were held in reserve behind Lala Baba. The disposition of our forces was as follows : One Brigade was ordered to attack Hill 70, another Brigade to attack Hill 112, with a third in reserve, while the divisions holding the trenches in the plain to the south were to rush the trenches in their front and then wheel northwards to converge on Hill 112 from the south.

THE ATTACK—HELL LET LOOSE !

By 2 p.m. Brigades had formed up behind such folds of ground as could be found on Lala Baba, and it became known that the infantry attack was to commence at 3.30 p.m., preceded and covered by a heavy bombardment from the fleet, which had drawn in-shore for the purpose, and which consisted of both battleships and cruisers, supported by several monitors.

This bombardment was to commence at 3 o'clock, and was to continue for two hours, our rôle being to advance at 4 o'clock, and move to Chocolate Hill, one-and-a-half miles distant, under the covering fire of the second hour's bombardment.

At 3 o'clock to the second every ship opened fire with her six-inch guns, the din being terrific. Every eye was strained towards Hills 70 and 112, and in a few seconds hell appeared to be let loose there. As the bombardment grew in intensity the hills became almost blotted from view, hid as they were in clouds of black and yellow smoke. Even at that distance it was easy to see masses of rock and earth being hurled skywards, and when rifts appeared in the smoke it seemed as if the hillsides were being blasted bodily away.

Although one could not hear their guns through the din, the enemy were evidently retaliating on Chocolate Hill and its immediate rear, as a white cloud, caused by bursting shrapnel, sprang into view above it and remained suspended there.

A bombardment such as this was a very much more imposing thing to watch, directed as it was against steep hillsides, than one of a similar density on the flat battlefields of France.

Before long, heavy rifle fire suddenly made itself audible, in spite of the heavy guns, and of great intensity it must have been to have been heard at all, telling us that the infantry attack had not only been launched, but that the Turks had by no means been obliterated or driven from their trenches, but, on the contrary, were putting up a big fight.

At this juncture orders came for the Division to fall in, preparatory to advancing. At 4 p.m. the leading Brigade commenced to move, and almost simultaneously the fire from the fleet died away, and we were thus bereft of the great moral and practical support derived from its covering fire.

INTO THE BARRAGE

On one side of our line of march lay the shallow, muddy waters of the Salt Lake itself, and on the other thick scrub, so that it was necessary for the Division to advance on a narrow front. The formation adopted was " Column of lines of troop columns."

To the uninitiated, it may be said that this formation is not quite so incomprehensible as it sounds ! Each squadron in the Division (and there were twenty-eight) followed the one in front, at a distance of approximately one hundred yards, whilst all the four troops of any squadron marched abreast, each in a short column of sections (*i.e.*, fours), and separated from the troop on its right or left by an interval of twenty yards.

The whole Division thus formed a column roughly one-and-a-half miles in length, the Notts & Derby Brigade being the rearmost. It was a magnificent sight to watch the Division unfold itself, like some gigantic serpent, as it defiled into the open. Until half-way across it seemed to be utterly ignored ; then suddenly the head became blotted from view by masses of upflung earth and clouds of black smoke, whilst the white puffs of shrapnel hung thick overhead.

From the rear one could watch squadron after squadron pass out of sight as it entered this barrage, but, beyond seeing the dispersal, or apparent obliteration of bodies of troops at the moment of entry, it was impossible to conjecture what was happening afterwards. All that one could see was that the men were behaving splendidly, that there was no halting or quickening of pace, and that all intervals and distances were being maintained as if on parade.

CHEERED BY THE WOUNDED

When one's own regiment met the barrage every officer there realised, as he had never done before, of what splendid material it was composed. The men literally did not seem to care one fig for the shells, nor had I ever seen them watch for and obey the least signal so promptly.   They seemed filled with a sense of elation, and would have gone anywhere and done anything.

Every enemy gun was concentrated on this narrow front, and very accurate shooting they made.   In so far as it was possible to judge, there seemed to be a series of some eight barrages, shrapnel and H.E. alternately. Whether this was so or not, of one thing I am certain, and that is that all that was necessary for a German gunner to do was to keep on loading and pounding at the same place to be sure of hitting something.

As a matter of fact, the barrages were not nearly so deadly as they looked.   Most of the shrapnel was burst either too high or too low, whilst a fair proportion of the H.E. was " dud."

It must not be supposed that the barrage was ineffective ; far from it.   The numerous dead, lying where they fell, were evidence to the contrary.

A number of wounded also had crawled to one side, and many of these were sitting up and cheering the column on, giving at the same time advice as to which bits of ground to avoid, if possible.

Amongst those we passed was Colonel Shepheard, commanding the Herts Yeomanry, who cheerfully informed us that he had got a comfortable " blighty one " through the leg, and would soon be on board ship, but that in the meantime we had best edge off a bit to our right for the sake of our own healths.   I deeply regret to record that the body of this gallant and popular officer was found later, a few yards from where we had seen him last.

TORTOISE IN THE BARRAGE

Whilst running this gauntlet the Regiment suffered the loss of several good N.C.O.'s and a number of men. I saw one shell knock out fully a dozen men in one troop, and within a few seconds overheard one of the few survivors pass a witticism of an uncomplimentary nature on a tortoise, which was making the best of his slow way out of the danger zone !   I recalled the

incident some weeks later when I found a dead tortoise
in exactly the same place, with a neat shrapnel hole
through the centre of his shell.

By 4 p.m., or soon after, the Regiment had crossed
the flat and reached Chocolate Hill, which on this side
was a slope of about 20 degrees; we were ordered to
lie down and wait, and as all the Division, with the
exception of one Brigade, were doing the same we
were pretty thick on the ground.

It did not take much intelligence for the enemy to
realise this, and from the moment of our arrival he
commenced to plaster it heavily with shrapnel.   Though
this inflicted a number of casualties, it was not to be
compared with what we had just been through, as
many of the shells either just caught the crest of the
hill or, carrying over, sprayed the flat ground immediately behind it.

On our arrival here we had our hopes dashed to the
ground on learning that the attack had failed to capture,
or rather to hold, Hill 70, whilst, of course, Hill 112
had not been attacked at all, the capture of the former
being essential to an attack on the latter.

Whilst waiting here, very heavy rifle fire broke out
beyond our hill, which we subsequently found out
was directed against the Bucks, Berks and Dorset
Yeomanry Brigade, who had made a magnificent charge
right up Hill 70, and had for a short time cleared and
held it.

THE PLAIN ABLAZE

Outflanked by machine-gun fire, they were forced
to retire, but later again made an equally fine assault
and, again, in spite of greatly reduced numbers, carried
the hill, only to be once more bombed and machine-
gunned off it.

Whilst this first attack was in progress we had
plenty of time to look at what was going on over the
ground which all had so recently crossed, and a terrible
sight it was, though, mercifully, the details were hidden
from our view.

Over the whole of the Salt Lake plain over which shelling had taken place the thick scrub had caught alight, and was now blazing furiously. In this scrub we knew many scores of wounded were lying, many unable to move. Some say that this was caused by incendiary shells, but I doubt it. The conditions were such that it was almost bound to happen in any case. Though nothing could be done in the way of rescue work, much was done by the stretcher-bearing parties, who had followed in rear of the Division, and, no doubt, many wounded were thus saved from a terrible death.

This wait behind Chocolate Hill had continued for nearly two hours, and had become exceedingly trying, especially as the excitement had died out of everyone, when an order was passed down that all commanding officers of our Brigade were wanted by General Kenna. Something was doing at last, and everyone felt thankful.

ADVANCE IN THE DARK

After a short absence, Colonel Lord Henry Bentinck returned and informed his squadron-leaders that the Brigade was ordered to attack what was described to him as a " communication trench, which was giving some trouble." The commanding officers had been pointed out the general direction, but had been unable to see the trench itself, owing to the darkness. All the information which it had been possible to give him was that it " was about 400 yards away over there " ! The South Notts Hussars were to head the attack, whilst the Sherwood Rangers and Derbys were to swing right and left handed respectively, and attack, whilst at the same time covering the flanks of the leading regiment.

The Brigade was hastily formed up in column of troops and moved clear of the right flank of Chocolate Hill, whilst direction was changed towards our objective. It was now nearly pitch dark. Once again it was impossible to give the men information or instructions.

Firing was going on in all directions, and bullets were pretty thick in the air ; where they came from it was quite impossible to say. To return the fire, even if it had been advisable, was out of the question, as no one knew whether our infantry were ahead of us or not. As a matter of fact, after the heavy gruelling which they had stood, during their attacks over rough ground, the infantry had perforce become broken up into small groups, each waging war, or not, on its own initiative, but one and all equally at a loss as to where they were themselves, or where the enemy were, whilst of our existence and entry into the fray they knew nothing. Readers will thus be able to gather that the attack opened with only the slightest prospect of success.

AT REAR OF TURKISH TRENCH

To show how mixed up things had become at this period, I will mention the case of Lieut. Swanwick, the regimental signalling officer, who, on returning from taking a message to Chocolate Hill, where Divisional Headquarters had been established, and seeking to rejoin the Regiment, found himself on the lip of a trench manned by Turks, which he had approached from the rear.   How he got there neither he nor anyone else could fathom.

During the advance in the dark the original orders were changed, and the Derbys were ordered to deploy to the left instead of to the right.   This order never reached " A " Squadron, with the result that they became detached, having held to the original instructions, and thus never took part in the actual attack.

I am unable, therefore, to give an eye-witness account of what happened, but it appears that the Brigade held straight on, every man still carrying the pick or shovel with which he had started in one hand, and his rifle with fixed bayonet in the other.

Their first intimation that they had approached their objective was a withering machine-gun and rifle fire at close quarters. This fire instantly killed Lieut.-Colonel Sir John Milbank, V.C., who was temporarily commanding the Brigade, and at the same time severely wounded Lieut.-Colonel Cole, the next senior officer.

Orders at this critical moment were in consequence not forthcoming, no one knowing in the darkness what had happened, and the Brigade in consequence came to a halt, which was natural.

The attack having thus lost its impetus, and as delay was impossible under the fire which it had to face, the only alternative was to retire. A short retirement was consequently made, a matter of some 300 yards, and it was probably just as well that it was made, as the so-called "support trench," which the Brigade was attacking, subsequently proved to be the main Turkish position—a double line of strong trenches close together, the second of which was timbered over and loopholed.

ABSENCE OF ORDERS

In the meantime, " A " Squadron had continued to the right, as originally ordered, thus losing touch. But on meeting only scattered groups of our infantry, none of whom could give any information as to the situation in that sector, direction was changed to the left, and after some searching a junction was effected with the remainder of the Regiment immediately after it had been compelled to withdraw.

About 300 men of the Brigade had been collected, and an officer was despatched to Divisional Headquarters at Chocolate Hill to obtain orders and to report. These orders were not forthcoming, as it transpired that H.Q. had retired to Lala Baba, after sending out runners to all units, ordering the Division to retire. As none of these runners ever reported, it must be presumed that they all either lost themselves in the darkness or were killed by snipers, or when crossing open ground, all of which was still heavily swept by rifle fire.

Five men were also sent to find water, and none of these were ever seen alive again.

In the absence of orders the Brigade commenced to dig themselves in where they stood, as retirement was out of the question until orders to do so were received. It was imperative to be entrenched before daylight, which was due in three hours, for it would then be impossible for anything to live above ground.

HIDING IN A DITCH

At this juncture an infantry officer reported that his men had captured a redoubt, and were urgently in need of reinforcements. " A " Squadron were accordingly sent out to locate it, and give what assistance was possible. A man was found who volunteered to show the way. On reaching a deep ditch, however, he stated that that was as far as he had been, but that he knew that the redoubt was at the end of it.

The squadron proceeded up this ditch in single file, crawling over the bodies of several men who had evidently been killed at the time of the original landing, until the ditch, which had been gradually growing narrower and more shallow, ceased altogether. At this moment a very heavy rifle and machine-gun fire broke out from all four sides.

There was no sign of the redoubt, and return being out of the question, owing to there being three hundred yards of open ground to recross, it only remained to wait where we were.

The fire was exceedingly heavy all the remainder of the night, making movement impossible, whilst with daylight a burst of heavy shell fire was heard to our immediate right. It subsequently transpired that this was directed at a small earthwork, which had been occupied by a troop under Lieut. Winterbottom, compelling him to retire, after losing heavily in proportion to his numbers.

With daylight, sniping started, one sniper, at least, being within a few yards and quite invisible. Excellent shooting he made, too, it being quite sufficient to show a finger above the ditch to have it hit. In addition to this, machine-guns were systematically sweeping every ditch and fence, and it was by the fire of these that Sergeant Elliott was killed.

ENFILADED BY TURKISH TRENCH

With daylight, it could be seen that we were within fifty yards or so of the Turkish trench, and enfiladed by it. In this predicament it was impossible to do anything but lie low, and hope to escape observation. This was exceedingly trying, and it was decided to try and rejoin our own lines by crawling back one by one under the best cover available.

Orders were passed down to the end of the ditch accordingly, but the first five men to make the attempt all chanced crossing a few yards of open ground, and were all killed by snipers. It was then decided to wait till nightfall. Firing was less heavy that night, and at 3 a.m. an opportunity occurred. A retirement was successfully accomplished, and the remainder of the Regiment were found holding a trench to our immediate rear.

I must here pay a tribute to the men. Before commencing the advance from Lala Baba on August 21st they had all been ordered to fill their water-bottles, but not to drink without orders. On rejoining on the early morning of the 23rd every man had still some water left, after being in action for forty hours in very hot weather.

Shortly after rejoining, the Regiment was ordered to hand over to the infantry and to return to Lala Baba, which we reached by 6 a.m. on the 23rd.

Everyone was about played out, having had practically no sleep since the night of the 20th, and certainly made the most of the few hours which they now got.

THE LOSSES

On the roll being called, it was found that our losses amounted to 78 out of 300, whilst the Division had lost somewhere between 1,200 and 1,500 out of less than 5,000 in action.

We heard that the total casualties for the engagement were well over 12,000—a large total, with no gain of ground whatsoever. This engagement may be said to have put an end to all the hopes of success which had inspired the Suvla landing. Depleted as all units were, and without hope of further reinforcement, it became obvious that in the future our rôle must, of necessity, be an entirely defensive one.

CHAPTER VI

GALLIPOLI—*continued*

TRENCH LIFE

ON the same evening, that is, the evening of August 23rd, the Regiment was again ordered up to Chocolate Hill, but on this occasion it marched under cover of dark, and arrived without incident. Here we rejoined the remainder of the Brigade, who were busily engaged in digging, and it was not long before we were doing the same.

As it was necessary to bivouac on the side of the hill itself, the flat ground at its foot being too exposed to shrapnel fire, the slope soon became a series of narrow terraces, some six feet in width. These were partitioned off by traverses at intervals of about eight feet, so that the hill became a mass of niches, tier above tier. Each niche contained, as a rule, four men, and though no head cover was possible, everyone was fairly secure so long as he lay close to his back wall.

No movement took place on the hill beyond what was absolutely necessary, as the whole hill was shelled fairly steadily, though not heavily for the first two days. The rest of the hill was equally crowded with other troops, and consequently there was a fairly steady flow of stretcher-bearers up and down it. Those who were killed were usually buried where they fell, if the spot happened to be exposed or unoccupied.

It was here, unfortunately, that the aptitude for digging of the Brigade, many of the men being colliers, was first discovered.

At first we took a pride in showing the infantry what Derbyshire and Nottinghamshire Yeomen could shift in the way of baked, brick-hard earth, but it was not long before we had every reason to repent us of our zeal. We found that having established a reputation we were expected to live up to it ! As weeks passed, the task never seemed to grow any less, although our numbers were decreasing the whole time.

On the 24th the officers and men who had not been allowed to take part in the action of the 21st rejoined us, and we were glad indeed to see them again, as by now we were four officers short. Captain Betterton and 2nd-Lieut. E. Gilpin had been wounded and evacuated, whilst Lieuts. Branfill and Keith had both gone down with bad dysentery.

EXPERIENCES WITH TURKISH SNIPERS

On August 26th the Regiment received orders to move the same night, and to occupy Azmac Dere, the dry water-course running down from Biyuk Anafarta, and a part of the second line which ran into it at right angles.

Lieut. W. B. Feilden, who was sent out during the afternoon to reconnoitre the ground over which the Brigade was to move to its new position, had a near shave, a sniper firing at him from a few yards' distance, and hitting his companion in the thigh. This officer had another narrow escape the same afternoon, immediately on his return to Chocolate Hill. He had just reached his niche, and his servant was handing him a cup of tea, when a shell arrived, blowing the latter's head off.

That night the Brigade moved to Azmac without incident.

During a short halt on the way a sniper nearly got me as I was lying down. I had just noticed that the bearer of a bright biscuit tin had deposited it close beside my head, and had just ordered him to remove it behind a tree, where it could not attract fire, when, before he could do so, a bullet skimmed my nose and, passing through the tin, hit its erstwhile bearer in the leg.

MAJOR A. A. SHUTTLEWORTH, T.D.

Commanded " B" Squadron on the outbreak of War.
Second in Command of the Regiment from 1915 until 1916.
Took Temporary Command of the Regiment, 1916

It would be possible to write pages on the subject of the Turkish snipers, who were most ingenious, as well as brave to a degree. For at least a week after the fight of the 21st there were many well behind our lines. These used to watch the few wells which existed, much as a big-game hunter might watch a water-hole.

Certain tracks to and from Chocolate Hill were exceedingly dangerous to traverse by day, in consequence. One sniper was annexed, and found to be rolled up in bundles of freshly-cut rushes. On another occasion two sand-bags, which had been lying motionless in the open for hours, commenced to crawl slowly away, but were stopped !

One day a small rationing party was fired on when going down to the beach. On their return they thought that the body of a dead Turk which they had passed on their outward journey seemed to be in a different position. They investigated by turning him over and trying to move his limbs, but found him perfectly rigid ; when, however, one enquirer tried the point of his bayonet, the corpse came very much to life—for the time being.

A GIRL SNIPER

It was reported that a girl sniper had been caught, and that on her were found no less than eighteen identity discs !

Spies, too, dressed in our uniforms, and talking perfect English, were undoubtedly numerous.

It was a matter of general belief, and not without ample grounds, that the Turks knew far more about any operation, or intended operation, than did those who were to play the leading part on the stage.

We had left Chocolate Hill none too soon, as early the following morning the enemy shelled it very heavily, having moved guns to a flank so as to enfilade it, killing and wounding, before breakfast, some seventy men of, I think, the Warwickshire Yeomanry.

At this period there were no communication trenches

E

between the front and support lines (where such existed), and it became our duty on reaching Azmac Dere to dig one from our position up to the front line, then held by the Sherwood Rangers, a matter of 600 yards. Although the ground was baked clay, and as hard as iron, the men were through with the job in three days' time.

On completion of this the Sherwoods were ordered to straighten their sector of line by digging a new trench in "no man's land," at an average distance of 150 yards beyond the trench they then occupied, which had been dug in the dark by the 10th Division, and which by daylight proved to be badly enfiladed.

This operation was most ably carried out, parties of our men assisting by driving through new communication trenches up to the new line. Unfortunately, before this could be driven through, the Brigade suffered a tremendous loss.

General P. Kenna, V.C., on the night of August 29th, insisted on seeing the new trench, and was mortally wounded whilst crossing the forty yards of open ground which separated it from the communication trench which was being driven through.

Every officer and man in the Brigade deplored the General's loss. Both as soldier and man he had won everyone's esteem and confidence. Though most of the senior officers had had their differences of opinion with some of the views he held, and adhered to, we all had eventually to admit that he had been perfectly right. Needless to say, his courage and personal disregard of danger had been an example to all.

Two days later the Brigade suffered another loss, this time in the person of Major Delmege, Brigade Major, a most popular officer, who was seriously wounded.

The Regiment, too, suffered several losses at this time, notably that of Squadron-Quartermaster-Sergeant Wright, who was very seriously wounded, and of

Quartermaster-Sergeant Holden, one of our most popular N.C.O.'s, who was killed by a shell whilst in the act of issuing rations to his men. Curious to say, though he was kneeling at the time, surrounded by men standing, not another man was touched.

This N.C.O. was buried close to where he fell, and as a rough cross was being placed over the grave the Turks fired a single round of shrapnel, which, bursting low, besprinkled the grave, but without touching two officers and two N.C.O.'s who were standing at its side.

All the time whilst on the Peninsula the Turks, or, rather, Germans, made most excellent sniping practice with their field guns. If more than two men got together outside a trench, or when going down to the beach to bathe, they would be certain to draw a round or two, which were almost invariably well aimed.

On occasions they used to extend this practice to the men who were actually in the water, and it was most amusing to see every man dive as he heard the shell approaching. I always think that the German gunners at Suvla Bay must have had the sport of their lives, and were probably the only people sorry to see us evacuate it.

ANOTHER ATTACK FAILS

On August 27th we witnessed a very heavy bombardment by the fleet on a hill (Hill 60), which lay to the extreme right of our front on the plain.

This was immediately followed by an attack delivered by an Irish Brigade, who advanced in two lines, their bayonets gleaming in the sun. They rushed the crest of the hill, disappearing beyond it, and out of our sight.

The Turks concentrated a heavy shell fire on the reverse slope, and this was followed by a bombing duel as the two sides came to grips.

The attack appeared to have succeeded, but just as everyone had started to speculate on the possibilities which the capture of this hill would open up, small groups of men again came in view, relentlessly pursued by a hail of shrapnel and H.E., and these could be seen dodging from cover to cover in an endeavour to re-form.

Many could be seen to fall, and then the scrub once more burst into flames, as it had done on the 21st, driving our men from that section of the hill. Yet another attack had failed with heavy loss.

IN THE LINE

On the night of August 30th the Regiment was moved up to the front line, *i.e.*, the new trenches which had just been dug, relieving, with the South Notts Hussars and two regiments of the London Mounted Brigade, the 6th and 7th Battalions Dublin Fusiliers. This brought the Regiment into line on the immediate left of the Sherwood Rangers.

On September 1st the Regiment was side-slipped to the right, taking over the trenches held by the Sherwoods, who were taken into reserve. This brought us to the left of the Ghurkas, though not into immediate touch with them, as a section of trench still remained to be dug, and to cut this section, and generally improve the new trench, was our first job.

Trench digging in Gallipoli was no joke. Not only was the work comparatively slow and extremely arduous, owing to the hardness of the ground itself, but it was frequently found, as on this occasion, that when all was progressing favourably someone would dig into a hastily buried body, which entailed filling in that section of trench, and making a detour.

All hands were turned to sand-bagging, widening, and improving the fire-step, etc. This lasted daily during daylight, whilst at night " A " and " B " Squadrons took it alternately to occupy the fire trench, whilst the other remained in the support trench fifty yards in rear. This trench, as I mentioned before, was the old front line, and was badly sited, having originated in the linking up of a number of short lengths of shelter trench, which had been dug in the dark and during an action.

SUPPORT TRENCH SHELLED

This trench, consequently, zig-zagged about in a weird way, some sections of it actually facing the rear, and, though for defensive purposes it was practically useless, it served us excellently a few days later.

The Turks on Hill 60 were able to see right down this trench, and the temptation must have been overwhelming, for one morning they shelled it very heavily for over an hour, using on this occasion captured French 75's. Though these proved far more alarming, owing to the sudden and unexpected arrival of their shells, than the Turkish fifteen-pounders, which gave one fair warning of their approach, very little damage was done.

This was entirely due to the fortunate chance which made this trench of such a tortuous character that almost every shell fell just where the trench should have been, but was not.

The fire trench, though excellent in itself, had a number of defects which were common to all the Suvla trenches. Although No Man's Land was 300 yards to 400 yards in width it was filled, for the most part, with dense scrub, or small half-cultivated patches of tall mealies, which not only prevented a good field of fire, but also served as excellent cover, should the enemy attack.

This would have been bad enough, even had we had the protection of wire entanglements, but these were conspicuous by their entire absence. Even if we had had the wire—and I never saw a coil of barbed wire whilst we were there—we should have been unable to use it, from lack of posts on which to affix it.

This absence of protection made dark nights a most trying time, for with darkness there came with great regularity heavy rifle and machine-gun fire from the Turkish trenches, and on occasions this might be described as furious.

THE CANDID "LISTENING POST"

Not knowing the way of the gentle Turk, this fire was at first expected to herald an attack, and everyone was consequently kept on the *qui vive*, and much valuable sleep was lost.

Later, however, one realised that this fire originated from jumpy nerves and fear of the dark and anticipated attacks on our part.

After realising this, we slept securely so long as the firing continued, in the certain knowledge that the enemy could not attack and shoot at the same time. But we awoke and became on the alert whenever the firing died down, and the silence became suspicious.

In the unavoidable absence of wire entanglements listening posts had to be relied on as the only means of protection.

At first, these were sent out singly or in pairs. When single, the listener was attached to a wire, which was intended to serve the double purpose of guiding him back and also as an indication of how far out he had gone. Personally, I often wondered whether the listener was lying down a few yards away, pulling in the wire hand over hand, in order to create a false impression of zeal.

I well remember that on the first occasion on which listening posts were used volunteers were called for. A notoriously sleepy and lethargic individual, who apparently knew not fear, was the first to come forward. On his reappearance at dawn next morning I seized the opportunity to deliver a " pat on the back," telling him how pleased I was to see his keenness, and asking him whether it was his desire to get on and win promotion that had prompted him to volunteer. His answer was candid, to say the least of it : " No, Sir, I thought if I went out I should get the chance of a real good *sleep*, and I had one ! "

To resume the narrative. We remained in these trenches, all continually digging, with the exception of those actually manning the fire trench or on ration fatigues, until September 4th, when we were relieved by the Sherwood Rangers, and retired to the reserve trenches at Azmac Dere. Unfortunately, just before we left the trench, Private T. P. Robinson, a most popular man, was badly hit in the head, and though able to walk down the trench for some distance, he shortly afterwards collapsed and died. I mention this incident to demonstrate the difficulty we always experienced in getting wounded men back.

PATIENCE AND COURAGE OF THE WOUNDED

At this time, the idea was that all trenches should be as narrow as possible, not only to save time where much digging was necessary, but also as protection against a direct hit, with the result that it was usually impossible to carry a stretcher down them. In spite of aid from the stretcher-bearers, who did magnificent work throughout, and were absolutely self-sacrificing, one and all, it was frequently impossible to get a dangerously wounded man down to the dressing station in time.

All this was unavoidable, and I feel sure that all ranks recognised it as such, judging from the manner in which they bore their wounds. The wounded were invariably cheerful, and would, I think, rather have bitten their tongues out than show any sign of suffering or complaint. To cite a few cases :

I remember one man, Private Hardy, being shot clean through the head when at a loophole on sentry. He "handed over" to his double (all sentries being worked in pairs), reported that he had been wounded, lit a cigarette, walked over two miles to the beach, and eventually recovered.

Private Hall (J. P., if I remember right), on being shot through the arm, dropped a fresh and laboriously made piece of toast, which he had been holding. He picked it up with the other hand, and ate it, remarking " that it was a good job it had'nt been a cup of tea," before going to the dressing station.

TYPICAL HEROISM

I remember no more gallant case than that of Private Burdett, and this I was told by the doctor in charge of the Brigade dressing station on August 21st.

This man came to the dressing station (a mud hut, through which bullets were passing fairly plentifully), having suffered a severe face wound. Without going into details, it was sufficiently bad to attract the doctor's attention, but on being told to come and have it dressed he refused to do so until several others had been attended to first.

After waiting for half an hour, he allowed himself to be attended to, and was just departing, the dressing having been completed, when the doctor asked him whether he had been hit anywhere else ?

" No," he said, " only a little one here," pointing to his stomach.

In spite of his assurance that it was nothing much, the doctor insisted on further investigation, and to his amazement discovered that poor Burdett had been cut clean open.

Nothing could be done for him, and he died in three days, without murmur or complaint.

Though a story such as this may sound horrible, and altogether out of good taste in a book, I am sure that it can inspire no feelings in his friends and relations other than of intense pride, otherwise I should not have mentioned it as typical of the heroism of the men.

We remained in the, so-called, rest trenches until September 7th. During this time all was comparatively quiet, though once or twice we were shelled, and it was at this time that Sergeants Holden and Wright were hit, as I have already mentioned.

During our short " rest," large working parties had to be continually found for digging trenches, and parties of officers and men were daily sent to Chocolate Hill, where an improvised bombing-school had been started. I think this course of instruction was cordially disliked by all.   Not only was the instruction given on an exposed piece of ground, which was very subject to shrapnel fire, but the walk to and from the hill was not without its dangers, one officer and several men being hit at various times on their way to receive instruction.

IMPROVEMENT IN SHOOTING

At this time the Brigade was re-formed into a " Brigade Regiment," under the command of Major Lance.   This Regiment consisted of three " double squadrons," with a total strength of possibly 600.

On September 7th the Regiment was moved up to relieve the South Notts Hussars in the fire trenches. Here once more every man not actually on sentry or fatigue was turned on to dig, officers doing their shift as well.   We only remained in this section until the 14th, during which time nothing unusual happened. Sniping was fairly bad here, and we had at least one sentry killed.

Owing to the thick scrub, it was impossible to keep down the sniping altogether, but nevertheless it had decreased enormously since the Brigade took over from the Dublins.

A few Turkish deserters kept coming in, and it was most gratifying to learn from them that the enemy had noticed a most marked improvement in the shooting immediately the Yeomanry came into the line.

This section of trench was comparatively sanitary, with the exception of a well, a few yards outside the trench, which contained five to ten dead bodies, probably those of men who had been sniped whilst drawing water during one of the earlier fights.

Sniping was at its worst at night, as it was then quite possible for Turks to creep up to the parapet itself, and to shoot at point blank range, and then wriggle away unseen.

" FRIEND, JOHNNY, FRIEND "

As an instance of this, a man of the Middlesex Yeomanry (who were on our immediate left), was standing on sentry one night at this time, with his rifle and hand resting on the parapet. You can imagine his feelings when his hand was suddenly, but firmly, grasped from out of the darkness, the grasp being immediately followed by the appearance of the body of a large Turk. Death appeared to stare him in the face, when, to his amazement, the Turk commenced to " pump handle " his hand in the most cordial of hand-shakes and to shout out " Friend, Johnny, friend," at the same time handing him his rifle over the parapet.

From prisoners we learned that their lot in the enemy trenches was a hard one—no pay for months, no leave, and only one biscuit a day, and that they hated their German officers, who were numerous. I fancy that this treatment was chiefly extended to those regiments recruited from Anatolia and Armenia.

It is certain that the Turks would have deserted in large numbers had they not had it firmly impressed on their minds that the British immediately hung all their prisoners. They would not have minded being shot, but seemed to draw the line at the rope. On discovering that we did neither, their surprise was unbounded, and frequent offers were made to go back and bring in their pals !

But for the danger of spies, this course would have been a most profitable and productive one.

On the 14th the Regiment was relieved by the Sherwood Rangers, and once more returned to Azmac Dere, where it was immediately turned on to dig a new communication trench.

OVERMUCH DIGGING

To illustrate how much digging formed the chief part of our existence, I will give a page out of the war diary at this period :—

September 14th.—Regiment relieved by S.R.Y. at 4.30 a.m., and moved to Azmac Dere. Commenced digging a new communication trench from the old to the new reserve trench, coming out at the Oak Tree.

September 15th.—Still at Azmac Dere, and engaged in various digging fatigues.

September 16th.—As yesterday.

September 17th.—As yesterday. At 9 p.m. the Regiment moved to new "rest" trenches, about a mile from Turkish line, the Brigade now consisting of the Notts and Derby Brigade and the London Yeomanry Brigade (each called Brigade Regiments), under the command of General Taylor, being relieved from the fire and support trenches by a Brigade of Scottish Horse.

[I may here add that the Scottish Horse, who had recently arrived, lost 250 men immediately on landing and whilst still on the beach.]

[The accommodation in the "rest" trenches was not sufficient for half the men, and it was necessary to dig hard till daylight to get cover for next day. The Regiment, as usual, dug splendidly. This meant a fair day's work, entailing, as it did, a whole day's digging in the reserve trenches, followed by a sudden move, always a wearisome and laborious job at the best of times, but infinitely worse with tired men, carrying not only their packs, but picks and shovels and all impedimenta down extremely narrow trenches in pitch dark, to be followed by a whole night's digging on baked ground, with the knowledge that you must be underground by day-break or be shelled to pieces.]

September 18th.—Regiment rested early in the accommodation made overnight, and later continued sapping to make more room.

September 19th.—Still improving trenches and making dug-outs. (We never had any material to roof them with, and they were no protection.) In evening formed fatigue parties to dig a communication trench to Brigade Head-quarters, General Wiggin having been wounded to-day when going to them.

September 20th.—Digging. A quiet day.

September 21st.—As yesterday. No shelling of our sector as yet.

September 23rd and 24th.—The men had a good rest, there being no digging between 9 p.m. and 9 a.m., and not much during the day.

ENEMY REFUSE TO LEAVE TRENCHES

During the afternoon of the 22nd the Turks opened a sudden and systematic bombardment, lasting for over an hour, and extending over the whole of our front, reserve and rest trenches, as well as over the communication trenches and the beaches. Everyone

expected an attack in force to follow, but nothing
whatever happened.

We subsequently heard that eight Turks had approached our trenches, and that they represented a
grand attack—the whole of the enemy having refused
to leave their trenches. Whether this was so or not
I am unable to say.

On September 25th the Regiment was moved into
the fire trenches occupied by the Queen's Own Westminster Hussars. This section of trench lay a few
hundred yards to the right, or south, of Chocolate Hill,
and a good half-mile to the left of those which we had
previously held.

We took over at 9.30 p.m., and were most disappointed
to find that our new line was not only very wet, as
well as being in a very dirty and insanitary condition,
but that it only contained one small sector of trench
at all, the major part of the line consisting of breastwork,
and this only one sand-bag thick, and therefore not
bullet-proof. Sand-bags being worth their weight in
gold, and therefore practically unobtainable, this was
no fault of the Q.O.W.H.

To entrench this sector was out of the question,
owing to the swampy nature of the ground and the
entire absence of pumps. I should not say " entire
absence," however, as there was one pump, but that
was badly broken.

Owing to the lack of sand-bags there was no parados,
and as one could only dig a foot or so before reaching
water, everyone in that sector had to live practically
in the open and in the utmost discomfort.

NUMBERS GETTING LOW

The outlook in front of this trench was no better
than that behind it. The ground had been heavily
fought over on August 21st both by the infantry and
by our own Brigade, and was in consequence still
thickly littered with dead, some of whom were quite
close to the parapet. At the time it had been quite

impossible to bury the dead, with the result that by the time about which I am writing the whole of this sector was in a most insanitary condition.

With the wind blowing towards us some sections of trench were almost unbearable. Latrines, and also cooking facilities for the men, were conspicuous by their absence.

Behind this sector lay neither support nor reserve trenches, nor were there any communication trenches to the rear.

Our numbers were now getting decidedly low and were quite insufficient to man the trench with any show of strength, and as this was weak in itself, apart from there being no support of any sort behind it, all hands had as usual to turn on and dig in order to provide greater protection and resistance.

HEALTH, FOOD AND FLIES

Before proceeding further with the narrative, I must say a few words on the above subjects, which were, after all, the ones which were most discussed in Gallipoli. Possibly, it was unavoidable that all three were bad.

For the first fortnight after we landed no fresh meat was issued at all, after which it began to appear occasionally, until eventually we received it, I think, twice a week. Vegetables, too, were entirely unobtainable at first. The first one which I tasted was a small onion, for which I gave a Sherwood " Tommy " 2s. 6d. This was some ten days after landing. Where he had obtained it I did not ask, else I might not have enjoyed the eating of it so much.

For the first fortnight or so our diet, in consequence, consisted of bully and biscuit—the large ones, the small round ones being regarded as a great luxury. I am afraid, too, that the tea and sugar of the iron ration became too great a temptation, and that the aforesaid " iron ration " was continually being consumed without authority. Variety of diet was in consequence impossible.

Wood was scarce, and water scarcer still, one quart per head for all purposes being allowed daily. As things began to settle down, dried potatoes and rice began to appear. These varied the monotony, but as the former could not be properly soaked, owing to the lack of water, and as it was impossible to wash out the starch from the latter for the same reason, I imagine that these two forms of vegetable did far more harm than good.

Maconochie rations began to be issued, and were immensely popular. Maconochie is distinctly rich, and I much doubt its being a good hot weather food. I may be doing Mr. Maconochie a great injustice, but I always noticed that an issue of his most palatable dish coincided with a rise in the sick report.

Later the rations became much better, jam and bread, to say nothing of margarine, being issued regularly. But I much doubt whether the very best of food would have kept the men in health, owing to the general conditions.

Water, apart from its shortage, was the chief cause of the initial trouble. Much was brought by ships, and this, though thick and not overclean, was probably good. A certain number of wells existed, and the water in some of these was passed as fit for consumption. Whether it was is another matter. Men had to have water, and all that the medical authorities could do was to condemn that which was obviously unfit. I doubt if there exists a single spring or well in the Gallipoli Peninsula which is not contaminated in some shape or form.

PARADISE OF BEELZEBUB

Washing, naturally, was a rare event, though occasionally water for this purpose could be obtained from wells which were not being used for drinking purposes.

When two or three men had to share half a biscuit-tin-full of the precious fluid for a bath—probably the first for weeks—discussion of a somewhat acrimonious nature was apt to run high. So much depended on whether an individual's face was dirtier than his hands, etc., etc., it being the golden rule that each should wash the cleanest part of his anatomy first, and then all proceed to the next cleanest. There is no need to labour the topic.

When in the " rest " trenches anyone not actually on a digging fatigue had the opportunity of walking down to the beach and having a delicious sea bathe. These little expeditions were not without their excitements, since if two of you going to bathe should meet two or three returning a shrapnel from the ever-watchful Turk would be pretty sure to arrive somewhere near the point of juncture.

I need say little about flies in this Paradise of Beelzebub !

A description is impossible. Everything in or near a trench seemed black with them, whilst at meal times their buzz rose to a positive roar. To eat a mouthful of food without eating one or more flies required the greatest skill and perseverance. Every mouthful on its way from the mess tin to the mouth became instantaneously black.

What sickened most people was to see men lying down in the trench bottoms in a sleep of exhaustion, with their mouths wide open, and these literally seething with flies.

One had only to remember the habits of the fly, the general lack of sanitary arrangements (disinfectants being very scarce), and the dead bodies over the parapet, to be thoroughly nauseated.

Of all the curses and plagues of Gallipoli, the flies easily held first place ; not only so, but they were probably the worst danger, and accounted for more dead than ever did the bomb, rifle or shell of the enemy. It was probably in consequence of the flies that even the smallest scratch or abrasion immediately festered or turned to blood-poisoning.

Under these conditions, *i.e.*, bad sanitation, bad

water, flies and extremely hard work, combined with a lack of fresh meat and vegetables, it was only to be expected that the health of the troops would suffer.

ON DUTY, THOUGH ILL

Up to this time sickness had not been greater than might have been expected, and though we had lost a certain number of men, who had been evacuated for strained hearts, etc., caused by constant digging, few had gone permanently sick from other causes.

Now, however, a very different state of affairs began to reign, for practically every officer and man began to suffer from acute diarrhœa. This after a short time usually turned to dysentery, or, failing that, to jaundice and troubles of a similar nature.

The doctors did everything possible with their limited equipment of drugs, but the sick returns nevertheless rose steadily. It was, of course, impossible to excuse duty to all who daily reported sick, otherwise there would not have been a man left to man the trenches, and it became the accepted thing for everyone to carry on whilst he had the strength left in him to stand up and hold a rifle during his term of sentry.

The men were perfectly splendid at this time, as always, and I know of many cases where men had literally to be ordered by their officers to report sick. I think that every man of the Brigade wanted to prove that he was the one who could " stick it " longest. Not only that, but everyone realised that for every man who went sick, and was evacuated in consequence, there would be a corresponding amount of extra work and duty thrown on the remainder.

As the numbers dwindled, the proportionate value of every man became progressively greater. The Brigade Regiment arrived in Gallipoli with a strength of roughly 1,100, and though by the time that it left the strength had dwindled to little over 300 it was still responsible for holding the same extent of front as it would have done had it been at full strength.

British Infantry

ANAFARTA

Asiatic hills beyond the Straits

hill 60

Buyuk Anafarta

← line held by Yeomanry Division

Chocolate Hill

SARI. BAHR

Gurka

hill 62

Australian and New Zealand

Southern half of Suvla Bay

Salt Lake

ANZAC COVE

Achibaba

LALA. BABA

CHELLES

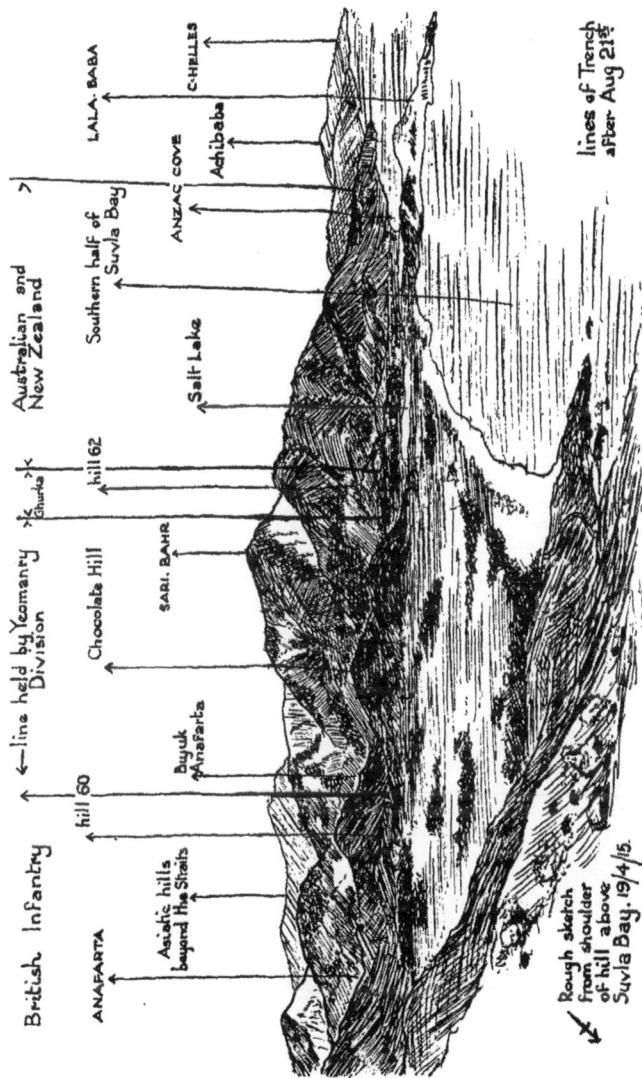

lines of Trench after Aug 21st

Rough sketch from shoulder of hill above Suvla Bay. 19/4/15.

In addition to this, very few of those who were still considered fit for duty were so in reality. Of the odd 300 left, 130 to 140 were parading daily for medical treatment, though still carrying on with their job, whilst of the whole number there were very few indeed who did not feel it a severe tax on their strength to carry their packs a matter of a few hundred yards, when moving from the firing line to the reserve trenches, or *vice versa*.

CHAPTER VII

GALLIPOLI—*continued*

VISIT OF SIR IAN HAMILTON

To pick up the threads of the narrative.

It is probable that the enemy noticed our endeavours to improve this section of trench, for on September 28th they shelled it on two occasions, causing a few casualties, amongst others poor Corporal Brooker, who died of wounds.

As a matter of fact, the whole Brigade had a very lucky " let off " to-day, though only a few senior officers knew it at the time.

On the 26th we were surprised to receive a visit in the trenches from the Commander-in-Chief, General Sir Ian Hamilton, and as this was the first time we had been honoured by his presence it was comparatively easy " to smell a rat."

The " rat " on this occasion took the form of a projected attack, which was to be delivered by our Brigade on the first favourable, *i.e.*, dark, night.   The plan of attack was to be kept with the utmost secrecy, commanding officers of the regiments concerned alone being in the know ; the only warning to be given was to be the issue of sand-bags for the attackers shortly before the attack was to take place.

Roughly, the attack was to be a converging one, carried out by the two Brigade regiments forming the Brigade.

The Turkish lines immediately opposite our sector formed a pronounced salient, protected at its apex by a thick overgrown swamp, and it was the intention to bite this salient off. The kicking-off point for our Regiment was to be an old ruined cottage which lay in our particular sector of trench.

We, who thought we knew, considered that the enemy trenches were held in strength, and that any attack over 400 yards of open ground, and delivered with a weak force, with no supports or reserves behind it, must mean little short of annihilation. The powers-that-be apparently thought otherwise, so that we were face to face with an attack similar to that on August 21st, in that both officers and men were likely to start off without any clear directions as to what was expected of them.

TURKS PREPARED

On the night of the 28th we were waiting about expecting to receive the order to attack, having received the sand-bags that afternoon, when a lucky chance knocked the whole thing on the head.

About 9 p.m. loud cheers were suddenly heard from the trenches held by Lovat's Scouts, who were on our right. No one had time to wonder what it meant, as almost simultaneously a terrific rifle and machine-gun fire broke out from the enemy trenches. At the same time two large bonfires which had been prepared by the enemy in the thick scrub of No Man's Land were lit, and the enemy artillery opened a heavy fire of shrapnel and H.E. This, curiously enough, was directed at the very spot at which we were to have left the trench, and was very accurate indeed. This was the only occasion on which I knew the enemy to use their guns at night.

The fire continued for forty-five minutes, and gradually died away, the Turk, I presume, being confident that he had annihilated everything living in the open, as he undoubtedly would have done.

After this, the attack was definitely " off," it being apparent that the trenches had been held, as we always thought, in great force.

What started the cheering ? Some wag suggested that a Scotchman had found a sixpence in a dead man's pocket. I believe this is an aspersion on the race, and that the real reason was the arrival of the news of our opening success at Neuve Chapelle, and the capture of 7,000 German prisoners.

Whatever the cause, we were grateful for it.

GERMANS WITHIN THE LINES

It is a significant fact that though the prospective attackers knew nothing as to the rôle which they were to play, and, except in the case of C.O.'s, did not even know that they had been cast for an attack, the Turks should have been fully prepared and awaiting it, even to the extent of having bonfires ready exactly opposite where we were to debouch from our trenches, and that this exact spot should receive a heavy and well-directed artillery fire.

The only conclusions which one could draw from this remarkable coincidence were not of such a nature as to inspire one with a feeling of confidence or security.

That there were Germans within our lines disguised as British officers was a well-known fact, and we received constant orders to look out for an officer of such and such a description. But that they should be able to pry out the most secretly formed plans was more than one liked to give them credit for.

On the 29th we were lucky in obtaining some sand-bags, and were thus able to provide rather better protection. The day was spent in sand-bagging, draining, making a central cook-house—as up to now each section of men had cooked for themselves—and digging fresh latrines. The latter gave constant employment, as under the existing conditions it was impossible to use the same latrines for more than a very few days.

On this day Lieutenant Swanwick, who had taken on the duties of Adjutant on Captain Brocklebank being attached to Divisional Headquarters, and who had for some time been literally hanging on by the skin of his teeth, was forced to go sick, and was evacuated, his place being taken by Lieutenant Johnson.

SILENCING THE TURKS

The Turks at this time were beginning to show more activity, and as their sniping was again becoming a nuisance, every man was ordered to fire five rounds during his half-hour's spell of sentry.

As these rounds had to be aimed either at some loophole in the enemy trench or at some possible lurking place of a sniper, and were fired under the observation of the N.C.O. on duty in each troop, the result was excellent. Not only did it soon reduce the Turk to comparative silence, but it at the same time gave our men confidence, and increased their morale, in so much that very soon they did not in the least mind how long they kept their heads above the parapet, even when being shot at.

I remember one man, and wish I could recollect his name, who, contrary to orders, had climbed out of the trench to improve the face of the parapet. Naturally, he immediately became a target, but continued with his self-imposed task until eight shots had been fired at him, and only climbed back after being hit in the hand and having finished his job, remarking, when reprimanded, that it would have been a pity to have left a good job half finished.

October 1st proved to be very foggy during the early morning, and the Regiment seized the opportunity to leave the trench and bury a number of our dead in No Man's Land. By this means a number of men who had been missing were identified both belonging to our own Brigade and to the infantry, the latter being mostly Sherwood Foresters.

These must have suffered heavily, and must have advanced with great determination. In one place I counted the bodies of twelve men with an officer in front, all lying on their faces in a perfect line and five yards interval. They must have been advancing as if on parade, till they met their death from machine-gun fire.

COLLECTING EQUIPMENT

As well as burying operations, which made life much more bearable in the trenches, the Brigade, whilst the fog lasted, collected and brought in a great quantity of rifles, ammunition and equipment. The Turks had evidently been round, too, for the boots of nearly all those we buried had been removed.

This morning was voted by all to have been " a most enjoyable one."

During the nights of the 3rd and 4th covering parties were provided by the Regiment whilst a communication trench was being dug to Pope's Sap. Probably the Turks were also out, digging in the open, as they did not molest the working party in any way.

At 9 a.m. on the 4th the Turks opened a very heavy fire on the trenches on our immediate right. The Regiment stood to arms, but, as usual, nothing came of the expected attack.

On this day, too, Lieut.-Colonel Lord Henry Bentinck, who had for some time been ill, but had nevertheless insisted on remaining on and doing an equal turn of duty with all his officers, was compelled by the doctor to go to hospital. Needless to say, his loss was keenly felt by all. During this trying time his devotion to his men, and his personal self-sacrifice on all occasions, had endeared him to all, and all were glad to hear of his recovery.

Major G. Strutt now took command.

Conditions remained much the same from now onwards, except that the strain on the men was gradually becoming heavier as their health deteriorated and their numbers decreased. The amount of work to be done, nevertheless, showed no signs of diminishing, but rather the reverse, as, in addition to the continual strengthening of the fire trench, we had been ordered to drive a long and deep communication trench back to the reserve line.

BOCHE AIRMAN PAYS THE PENALTY

The weather remained hot and dry until October 8th, when we were relieved by the Bucks Hussars, after being in the fire trenches for a spell of thirty-two days. That night it poured with rain and was bitterly cold.

From this date until the Brigade was withdrawn from the peninsula, on November 1st, we remained in reserve, during which time the Regiment was ordered, on several occasions, to provide large covering parties to protect digging parties, which were preparing a forward trench system in advance of our old fire trench.

On October 9th, Lieutenant Johnson went sick, thus reducing the number of officers to three—Lieutenant Chetwynd, Lieutenant W. Feilden and myself—the total strength of the Regiment now being 120.

During this period, in the reserve trenches, we were shelled spasmodically, and had to keep our heads low after dark, as it was found that the siting of the trench coincided with the strike of bullets which passed over the parapet of the fire trenches. But apart from this we had no excitements, except those provided by aeroplanes.

On two occasions a plucky Boche airman carried out very low reconnaisances, diving down and flying the whole length of the trenches at the height of not more than fifty feet. He naturally had to face a terrific rifle and machine-gun fire, and on his second visit was hit and eventually crashed out of our sight behind his own lines.

On another occasion one of our own planes provided the excitement. When at 9,000 feet, and well behind the enemy lines, its diving gear jammed, necessitating a forced descent. It appeared as if it must land behind the enemy trenches, but just cleared them, being fired at by everything which the Turk could bring to bear. It literally skimmed our trenches, and took the ground in the mud of Salt Lake.

Turkish field guns immediately opened fire, and made

remarkable shooting, hitting it with the third or fourth
shot, and at the same time making what seemed very
close shooting at the two airmen, who were ploughing
their way, in thick deep mud, back to Lala Baba,
but without hitting them.

PRACTICE AT FLYING GEESE

Every morning now there appeared large flocks of
geese and storks winging their way south. They were
the envy of every man on the peninsula. As it was
impossible to grow wings, we one and all, the Turks
included, loaded our rifles when we heard the " honk,
honk " in the distance. The fire which greeted their
arrival would have annihilated an army corps, but, to
the best of my recollection, it only brought down
one stork.

For weeks past we had been hoping for reinforcements
for the Brigade from Egypt. But our hopes were
dashed to the ground when we heard, in mid-October,
that a composite regiment had been formed from the
three squadrons which we had left behind in Cairo,
and that it had been despatched to Salonica to co-operate
with the 10th Division, which had recently been withdrawn from Suvla, in the original landing at that place.

LEAVING THE PENINSULA

Shortly after this, General Peyton informed a meeting
of the senior officers of all regiments in the Division
that, owing to lack of reinforcement, the Division,
which now had roughly only 1,200 left of the 5,500
who had landed in Gallipoli, would be shortly withdrawn.

This was eventually carried out on November 2nd
and 3rd. The Notts & Derby Brigade were embarked
on the *Hermione* at 6.15 p.m., and were landed at
" Turks' Head " pier at Mudros.

There were now only two officers left with the
Derbys—Lieutenants T. Chetwynd and W. M. B.
Feilden—for Major Strutt had gone sick on the 1st.
I have no record of the actual number of men who

finally left, but what there were narrowly escaped suffocation when being evacuated on lighters. They were crowded below deck by the disembarkation officers, and the hatches placed on, owing to a choppy sea, and when these were removed several of the men were literally at their last gasp.

Soon after landing, a good many men went sick, or, I should say, went to hospital, for they had most of them been sick for weeks. Lieutenant W. M. B. Feilden also had to give in, but the situation was relieved by the arrival of Captain N. D'Arcy Clark and 2nd-Lieutenant R. O. Feilden from Salonica, and Lieutenant G. Jackson and 2nd-Lieutenant Calder from the 2nd Line Regiment in England.

BACK TO EGYPT

The Regiment had a trying time in Mudros, as it had to stay there until November 25th before embarking on the *Themistocles* for Alexandria, and during this time suffered several disappointments, owing to embarkation being postponed on account of bad weather.

On November 6th Sergeant-Major Gillett received his commission in the Regiment. This was the first commission given to an N.C.O. in the Regiment, and no N.C.O. ever earned it better. Lieutenant Gillett, whose death from malaria in Salonica we later had to deplore, was one of the most popular N.C.O.'s, both with men and officers, that it has been my good fortune to meet. During our time in Gallipoli it was most remarkable how this N.C.O. succeeded in keeping his men's spirits up when everyone else was feeling depressed. His death in 1918 was a great loss, not only to his many friends, but to the Regiment.

On November 28th the Regiment reached Egypt, and was entrained for Cairo, reaching Mena Camp, near the Pyramids, the same night.

Shortly before the Regiment left Mudros it received the news of Captain Lord Vernon's death at Malta from dysentery. Lord Vernon was universally popular, and there was not an officer or man in the Regiment who did not feel, and rightly, that he had lost a real friend.

PADRES AND RUMOURS

Before finally closing the portion of this history dealing with Gallipoli, I wish to add a few notes which should have found their proper place earlier.

Everyone who was there will join with me in a tribute to Father Day and the Rev. F.(?) Bevan, the Catholic and Protestant priests attached to the Brigade. How much they achieved will never be known, but this I do know, that it was a common sight to see men who had previously never given religion a thought deeply poring over a Bible or Prayer-book in the trenches. Not only that they did untold good by their example of personal courage and fortitude ; they were always amongst the men, cheering them up when they most needed it, and really getting a hold on them owing to their broad-mindedness and tolerance of what I might call " trench language."

They will forgive me if I refer to the many, I fear totally unfounded, rumours which they circulated, many of which would have shamed the *Daily Excess* : " We are through the Dardanelles," " The Turks have asked for an Armistice," " The Germans have retired all along the line," etc., etc. When these proved to be unfounded, a certain and safe antidote to the disappointment was always ready to hand : " There will be some wonderful news announced in three days' time "—and then another rumour.

These rumours spread like wild-fire, and though no one really believed them, they most certainly served their purpose.

That the Medical Officers did all that lay within their power under the most adverse circumstances goes without saying, and if at first one did get a Number 9 instead of a Number 4, what matter ! It was probably all they had to give !

ASIATIC ANNIE'S MISSILES

I could say a lot on the subject of guns, both Turkish and British. The former, when once we were entrenched, did singularly little harm, and caused a certain amount of interest and, at times, even amusement, whilst the latter were conspicuous by their absence. Many of the heavy Turkish guns, several of which were sited on the far side of the Straits, became quite old friends and were known by somewhat intimate nicknames.

Every morning, whilst in the Chocolate Hill trenches, we would await the slow and leisurely arrival of " Asiatic Annie's " missiles. The first of these invariably arrived at 9 a.m., followed at intervals of three or four minutes by nine or ten others. These were always directed at the same target—a couple of our howitzers at the base of Chocolate Hill.

There was always some speculation about the first arrival, in case it should be a short, and land in our trench, 400 yards in advance of the guns. One or two nearly did, but never quite, nor did they ever quite hit the guns, to my knowledge.

Besides these two guns, I believe we had one or two somewhere near " A " Beach. There certainly were some half-dozen on Lala Baba, and an odd 4·7 or so amongst the sand dunes to the south of it. Possibly, behind the Suvla Army, excluding Anzac, there may have been a round dozen guns on shore, but I much doubt if we ever had so many fit for action at one time.

Concrete emplacements had been prepared for four heavy howitzers, and though the crews of these were landed, the guns themselves never got further than Mudros.

The chief difficulty about guns, apparently, was the almost total lack of possible gun positions. Had these been more numerous we should doubtless have had more guns.

Besides these shore guns, we, of course, had the

backing of the fleet, whose guns, when they did fire, made a terrific noise, but were otherwise of little value, as it was howitzers, and not high velocity guns which were required.

SEARCHING FOR "BLISTER BOTTOMS"

The monitors and "blister bottoms" caused never-ending interest. Most days one of these would be seen to steam from round the point of Lala Baba, hover around for half an hour, and finally come to rest and commence firing. Awe-inspiring portions of cliff or hill side would fall away, containing, we hoped, many Turks, and then presently a distant hum and rumble would be heard, which immediately caused every glass to be turned on the "blister bottom," to see the sighting shot of the Turks' reply.

This was usually somewhere around the objective, and would cause it to get under way—a very slow way, usually—and prowl round for half an hour, whilst the Turk continued to shell the Aegean until tired, after which the "blister" would resume operations.

On one occasion the Turk gave the fleet, who were lying too close inshore, quite a hot time, and the *Royal George*, I think it was, was hit frequently. They had to clear hurriedly, and we on shore were secretly very pleased, as we always had the feeling that the fleet might have been more lavish with their ammunition or, at least, if that were impossible, might have asked one off to lunch. We should have preferred the latter to a man.

TRACES OF EARLY CIVILISATION

Agriculture, as we found it, was of a most primitive nature, and could have developed little since the time of ancient Troy.

Traces of an early and highly civilised population there were in plenty, and several finely carved marble slabs and coffins, presumably, were dug up. On these were inscriptions in the Homeric style, setting forth the pedigree of the deceased.

Numerous scraps of pottery were unearthed whilst
digging trenches, and as these were usually found at
a depth of four or five feet, it must be presumed that
at that time the peninsula must have stood at a considerably higher level than it does now, for nowhere
were we more than a few feet above sea level.

As to trench life the general rule was for one squadron
to be on duty in the fire trench for twenty-four hours
with the other squadron in reserve and *vice versa*.
Latterly, however, owing to the paucity of numbers,
it became necessary for both squadrons to be on duty
in the front line at the same time, and this for weeks
on end.

Life under these conditions became very trying, as
no rest was obtainable. Sentries were always employed
in pairs, the spell of duty lasting an hour, one man
being on the fire-step, with the other sitting close to,
on the alert.

As each " bay " had to have one double sentry,
and, as men were few and far between, each man had
to be on sentry for one hour out of every three, both
by night and day. Had it been possible for him to
have had the two hours off, duty free, to rest in, all
would have been well, but this was quite out of the
question, as rationing parties and numerous digging
parties had to be provided.

For one hour before dawn all troops in the front line
had to stand to arms, and this further spoiled what
little chance of rest one had. During the night officers
took two-hour watches, during which time they had
to be perpetually on the move up and down the trenches,
in order to see that all reliefs of sentries were properly
carried out. When the number of officers became
reduced to three or four, this duty became trying, to
say the least of it.

SNAKES AND ANIMAL LIFE

The animal life of Gallipoli also deserves a word of
mention. No! I am not referring to the animal life

of a somewhat personal nature, from which we all suffered, but to the larger varieties. It was a most interesting experience to pass down a newly-dug trench. Such trenches acted as a sort of trap, cutting, as they did, through the runs of rats, mice and the like. During their nocturnal wanderings, these would suddenly find themselves falling over a precipice, with the result that the floor of the trench would be covered with scores of them in the morning.

Rats were comparatively scarce, but mice of several varieties were abundant. In addition to these, snakes of at least five varieties were frequently found, varying in size from a foot up to one monster of five feet, which put up a great fight before being slain. Some of these were extremely venomous.

Other animals which found their way to the trenches were small green tree frogs and baby toads by the hundred. For some time I kept one of the former and three of the latter in my dug-out for company's sake.

On one memorable occasion, a brown hare fell into the trench, and found his way from thence to the pot in record time.

During the Regiment's stay on the peninsula it received no reinforcements, with the exception of eight men who were returned from hospital at Mudros, after being wounded on August 21st. These gave a deplorable account of the conditions there. One of these, Sergeant Brough, had a curious experience. He was hit in the head and knocked senseless ; on recovering, he heard something rattle in his helmet, and on taking it off out dropped the bullet, which had fractured his skull without penetrating. Unkind friends naturally had a good deal to say on the subject !

A CLEAN FIGHTER

No gas was used on either side from start to finish, and I think all agreed that the Turk fought cleanly and honourably. Of his courage there was never any doubt. He lacked material, which was fortunate for us. Had he had aeroplane bombs and artillery ammunition in any quantity our stay in Gallipoli would have been limited to days, and the same may equally well be said for us.

The Suvla landing ended in utter failure and heavy loss, but left no blot on the nation's history. That this was so is due to the dogged pluck and perseverance of the men, and not to any Government department.

For how much the brains of the expedition were responsible, history will some day show. Had the original landing been made with well-trained troops, who knew what was expected of them and exactly what they were to do, and had these been backed up, as they should have been, with guns, bombs, reinforcements and supplies of all sorts, especially medical, the termination would have been very different. The expedition could and would have been justified.

If those responsible knew that such supplies of men and munitions would be unavailable, they accepted a responsibility which no man was justified in taking. Had Gallipoli been nearer England, and under the direct eye of the Press and the public, a very different chapter would have been written and many lives gallantly and fruitlessly given would have been spared.

Probably the Turkish army was in the same predicament, for had they had food and munitions, and had they at the same time shown initiative, few British troops would have returned from Suvla otherwise than as prisoners of war.

CHAPTER VIII
The Senussi

Whilst the Regiment was waiting in Mudros for transport to Egypt a new campaign had been inaugurated in that country, namely, what was usually known as the " Senussi Show."

The Senussi is the title of the chief of a nomad tribe living on the frontier of Tripoli. This tribe was of a very warlike nature, and had become paramount amongst the other frontier tribes, who not only recognised its suzerainty, but became known under the name of Senussi themselves.

This tribe had a great war record behind it, and proudly claimed never to have been beaten in battle. Certain it is that when the Italians sent punitive expeditions against them, the latter were badly beaten, and were compelled to retire to the coast, leaving the Senussi undisputed masters of the interior and of a considerable section of coast line as well.

The British, on the other hand, entered into a friendly agreement with the Senussi, whereby they bound themselves over to keep the peace, whilst we, for our part, delivered to them periodically convoys of food-stuffs and necessities.

This arrangement worked well for a number of years, and to our mutual advantage, until the Great War broke out.

GERMAN PROPAGANDA AMONGST NATIVES

It soon became evident that German propaganda had not left this stone unturned, and that there was a distinct change in the feeling of the tribes.

MAJOR D'ARCY CLARK, T.D.

Commanded "C" Squadron (Old "D" Squadron). Second in Command, 1917, until termination of the War. Brought Cadre of the Regiment home in 1919

At first sight it may appear that there could be little to fear from this direction, but one only has to remember that we had deposed the Khedive, and taken away the suzerainty of Egypt from the Turks, setting up a Sultan of our own nomination in 1914, that Egypt was, in consequence, full of sedition and Turkish sympathisers, and was therefore a hotbed of German propaganda, to realise that any war-like native force on the western frontier was capable of untold harm.

Up to now we had maintained no regular force, excepting the Egyptian coastguard mounted patrol service, nor was one necessary, as we appeared to have no potential enemy.

Egypt's defence on this front was her desert, but in this desert lay several groups of oases, the possession of which would give an enemy a gateway into the country which would be extremely hard to wrest from him.

A MYSTERIOUS TRIBE

Both in the European and native mind had sprung up a feeling of mystery as regards these tribes, or, rather, as regards the tribe of the Senussi himself. It was popularly supposed that no European had ever seen him, that the tribe were almost white, that he had a body-guard clothed in armour of gold, whilst his army were equipped like that of the old Saracens and Crusaders.

Such beliefs were guaranteed to make a great impression on the minds of the Egyptian natives and Bedouins, and it was confidently expected that if the Senussi should declare a holy war he would have the immediate support of the whole of the discontented Mahommedan population in Egypt.

Our forces at this time, that is, November, 1915, were small, with the exception of the army which was fully occupied in the area of the Suez Canal. The fighting in Mesopotamia had assumed large proportions, Gallipoli had not yet been evacuated, whilst we had

G

only recently launched forth on the Salonica venture,
and there were few troops to be spared from home,
and none from France.

Matters came to a head in mid-November. The
Senussi were known to have received both field and
machine-guns through German agencies, and they now
made hostilities imperative by attacking Egyptian
coastguard patrols.

For operations on our part to have any success
mounted troops were an absolute necessity. Apart
from a regiment of Australian Light Horse, the only
cavalry in Egypt consisted of details of the fifteen
regiments forming the 2nd Mounted Division, now in
Mudros. These details, for the most part, consisted
of the sick and wounded from Gallipoli, who had been
returned for duty from Mudros, Malta and Alexandria.

A REMARKABLE BRIGADE

Out of these a composite Mounted Brigade was
hastily formed on November 18th and 19th. The
regiment, which included the Derbyshire Yeomanry
contingent, was formed of the odds and ends of at
least six other Yeomanry regiments. I was in hospital
in Cairo at the time, and was in consequence unable
to go, but Lieutenants Branfill, Keith and Allsebrook
were more fortunate than I.

It must have been the strangest brigade which was
ever formed for immediate offensive operations. Any
officer appears to have been given almost any command
for which he liked to apply, and, of course, neither
men nor officers knew one another. Lieutenants usually
found themselves commanding squadrons, and I heard
of one squadron which contained details of no fewer
than twelve regiments. However, they did their job,
and did it well, as everyone knew they would.

When the Brigade marched from Mena Camp, and
entrained at Cairo on the 19th, we who were left and,
indeed, the whole of the European population of Cairo,
felt singularly deserted and unprotected. As I was

unable to accompany the expedition I am unable to write as an eye-witness, and the following short account of the chief incidents which happened to the regiment containing the Derbyshire contingent, is from information supplied by Lieutenant Keith.

The period covered extended a little over one month, as at the end of that time the Derbyshire contingent were recalled to rejoin the Regiment, which had then returned from Mudros.

The regiment of which the Derbys formed part entrained at Cairo on November 19th, and after being taken down to the coast, eventually found itself in bivouac at Jamum, not far from the railhead at Dabaa, which is about a hundred miles west of Alexandria.

THE DESERT DUST STORMS

Here they remained until December 5th, being employed in forming an outpost line, behind which other troops were being concentrated, and also in continual desert patrols, some of which were of considerable interest.

Here, too, they discovered at first hand the difficulties and annoyances of desert warfare. Water was a great difficulty—there was little for the men, and practically none for the horses, and what little there was was bad.

This was bad enough, but what made matters worse were the dust storms, one of which lasted for twenty-four hours on end. For the benefit of those who have not experienced a dust storm in Egypt, I wish to explain that they must dissociate their minds entirely from the sort of dust storm which one meets in a country road in England.

The dust storms of the desert are composed of dense clouds of hot, rough sand, mixed with a fair proportion of moderate-sized pebbles. This is usually driven by a raging wind, often sufficient to uproot every tent, leaving one unprotected and totally unable to open one's eyes. Any equipment left on the ground is instantly buried, and usually that which is of most value to one absolutely defies one's efforts to recover it by digging.

The sand penetrates everywhere and everything, and eating becomes next to a physical impossibility.

The horses naturally suffer intensely.

On December 5th the Notts Horse Artillery Battery joined up with the regiment and, accompanied by a convoy of a mile-and-a-half in length, the column commenced a long desert march of a hundred miles due west along the coast to Mersa Matruh. The Yeomanry during this march had, of course, to do all the advance guard work by day and the outpost work by night. Here, again, water proved to be the greatest difficulty, but the trek, nevertheless, was described to me as a most interesting one.

AN INTERESTING TREK

On our approach, the Senussi had all cleared out from this part, having doubtless gone to make their own concentration, but from what I gathered they had been unable to take their household goods with them, and as it was the obvious duty of any advance guard to search every house which could have contained the enemy or their spies, the " interest " of the trek is, I think, accounted for. After all, it would have been a pity to have left any object of value lying about to be stolen by the infantry !

During one stretch of fifty miles there was only one well, and that contained very little water. Fortunately, the Australian A.S.C. had brought some thousands of gallons along with them, which eked matters out, but, even so, there was little enough for the 1,200 horses which were in the column.

Mersa Matruh was reached on the 8th, and men and horses were given a two days' rest, of which they were not sorry to avail themselves.

Mersa Matruh possessed a good harbour and also a strong defensive position on the land side, and was accordingly chosen as the advanced base of the operations.

ATTACK ON THE SENUSSI

On the morning of the 11th, at 5.30, to be precise, some 400 of the enemy were reported to be encamped eight miles south-west of Matruh, and the composite regiment was accordingly moved out, accompanied by two guns and six armoured cars.

The going was across more or less open desert, and was flanked on the right by a chain of rough hills.

After covering about four miles, the advance and right flank guards were fired on from these hills, and shortly afterwards the enemy were seen freely moving about in a position which they had evidently taken up with the idea of holding.

The two guns were immediately unlimbered, and opened fire on this position, whilst the Yeomanry and armoured cars endeavoured to outflank it.

This movement failed, as on approaching the hills the going became worse and worse, changing from desert sand to rough stones and boulders. The Yeomanry were consequently compelled to dismount, and to engage the enemy on foot.

One charge was, however, delivered, and met with complete failure, a number of casualties being sustained. This was entirely due to the nature of the ground.

The scene lay between two spurs of the hill, and as the charging squadron advanced between these, they found themselves in what may be described as a bottle-neck, and the further up the neck they went the rougher the ground became, and the slower the pace ; which eventually declined to little more than a walk.

As the enemy had machine-guns at the end of the neck, and as our front had perforce become contracted, our men provided an excellent target, and though the leading troop did, I believe, actually reach the enemy, the charge was broken.

SMALL PARTY CUT OFF

I believe I am right in saying that it was soon after, and in consequence of this charge, that Lieutenant

Allsebrook found himself surrounded by the Senussi. He had only nine Yeomen with him, a totally insufficient force with which to cut his way out. Taking up a position in a small cup-shaped hollow, surrounded with boulders, he tied his horses " head and tail," so as to leave every man available for fighting, and for the next four hours had a very lively time of it.

There fortunately were only one or two ways by which the enemy could get within the circle, and by careful shooting at these on each occasion when a Senussi showed himself he managed to avoid being rushed, and maintained a strong defence, killing a number of the enemy and being himself wounded in the head, until relieved by, if I remember rightly, an armoured car.

After four hours' fighting the main body of the enemy retired, but, owing to the presence of a deep ravine, the Yeomanry were unable to follow them up, and the engagement was consequently broken off. At 8 p.m. the column got into camp at Armrakoum, which is about eighteen miles west of Matruh, both men and horses being very tired.

In the meantime, the rest of the force had been joined by some infantry, namely, a battalion of Sikhs and another of Royal Scots.

On the following day, December 12th, our aeroplanes reported a large force of the enemy approaching from the south-west.

At 6 a.m. on the 13th the whole force was got under arms and moved out without delay. The formation adopted was a fan-shaped one, with the mounted troops forming the advance guard, the Australian Light Horse on the right, and the Yeomanry on the centre and left.

After marching about five miles in the direction in which the enemy had been reported, the advance guard were suddenly heavily fired on along the whole front.

AUSTRALIANS' EXCESSIVE ZEAL

The Australians appear to have shown an excess of zeal, for every man immediately dismounted and opened rapid fire, quite forgetting their horses, who went off anywhere and everywhere. The Australians having thus committed themselves to a dismounted action, the Yeomanry were compelled to conform accordingly, and came into dismounted action on their left, with the Sikhs on their left, and the Royal Scots beyond them.

A heavy action ensued, and all went well until the ammunition of the Australians began to run short, thus compelling them to withdraw towards the coast and the edge of the cliffs above it.

In the meantime, the Royal Scots had also been compelled to fall back to the cliffs, thus leaving both flanks exposed.

A steady fire was kept up on the advancing enemy until midday, when Colonel Gordon, commanding the column, ordered the Yeomanry to withdraw and to conform with the new line. This was successfully carried out.

The Sikhs were thus left " in the air," and practically isolated. Their tactical position was extremely weak, though their ground position was a strong one.

Although a mile in front of the line, this gallant regiment maintained a magnificent defence, and, though heavily pressed, never yielded an inch of ground. This state of affairs lasted until 3 p.m., when matters had assumed a rather critical position, for the ammunition of the Yeomanry, who were engaged on the flank, had now become almost exhausted.

A TIMELY ADVANCE

At this juncture, and none too soon, the Royal Scots again advanced from under cover of the cliffs. The advance was made at the double, and was aimed at turning the right flank of the enemy. This succeeded with very little fighting, as the enemy seem to have regarded this as a fresh force which had been held in reserve, and promptly withdrew his threatened flank.

This left the Sikhs free to withdraw from their perilous position, and they again came into line with the Yeomanry above the edge of the cliffs, thus once more reuniting the whole force.

At 7 p.m., after thirteen hours of heavy and continuous fighting, the force was withdrawn under cover of darkness, and made the best of its way back to the camp, nearly five miles away.

An attack on the camp was fully expected, and the troops spent a rather sleepless night in a circle round it.

Why the enemy did not attack us here, when we were exhausted and out of ammunition, it is hard to say; but, probably, he was in the same condition himself, or, like most natives, disliked night fighting. Whatever the reason, he missed a great opportunity.

At 5 a.m. the force commenced to retire, falling back on Mersa Matruh. The movement was successfully carried out, for the Senussi only discovered it too late, and in time only to fire a few shots at the rear-guard.

A short stay was made at Mersa whilst reinforcements were arriving, and on Christmas Day this greatly strengthened force made a fresh attack on the enemy near the scene of the engagement of the 13th.

This time our attack met with complete success, and a severe defeat was inflicted on the Senussi, who lost several hundreds of men and a great number of camels. To a nomad army like theirs, the latter was undoubtedly the severest loss of the two.

I have no particulars of the engagement.

TRAITOROUS ATTACKS

In both these actions the enemy made use of machine-guns and also of several mountain guns, but with these they made very poor practice. During our advance on the Christmas Day fight, the Senussi showed that he was unused to the methods of civilised warfare, for it was the general custom of both wounded and unwounded to sham dead, and to seize the nearest rifle and shoot into the backs of our men after they had passed them.

Cases, too, occurred of men being shot, or stabbed, by wounded Senussi whilst giving them a drink of water. This was so much the worse for the enemy, as, after losing a number of men in this way, the only possible remedy was adopted.

The hills abounded with caves, and into these the enemy in twos and threes fled for hiding, and were duly ferreted out by our men.

There were many amusing stories in connection with minor attacks on caves, but only one, which seems to have afforded considerable merriment, affects the Derbys.

CAVE INCIDENTS

Lieutenant Branfill, who had displayed great gallantry during all the operations, had marked down for himself a certain cave, into which he had seen a Senussi enter, after leaving his camel outside. Possibly, he did not wish to annex the camel without first asking permission of the owner, but as he was seen to enter the cave, revolver in hand, the reason of his entry must remain a mystery.

What happened in the cave history does not recount, but of his exit there is no doubt. This was sudden, and of a somewhat hurried nature, for in his wake rushed a Senussi, armed with a stupendous elephant gun. How Lieutenant Branfill overcame the foe is another story.

Perhaps it will be unkind to relate how Lieutenant Keith tried to shoot a Senussi in the head at short range with his revolver, and how he hit him in the foot instead. That he killed him with his sixth shot is, I believe, a fact, but then, as he admits, " the Senussi were remarkably tough."

This action was the last in which the Derbyshire contingent took part, for by this time the remainder of the Regiment had received drafts from England, and were re-forming at Mena Camp, near Cairo, and they received orders to rejoin their unit, which they did about January 1st.

THE REGIMENT RE-FORMS

The remnants of the Regiment left from Gallipoli reached Mena Camp, which is close to the Pyramids, on November 28th. Whilst they had been at Mudros reinforcements to the number of about two hundred had arrived from the Second-Line Regiment in England. At Mena also were a few details who had not gone on the Senussi expedition, owing to sickness and other causes, and with these three bodies, and allowing for those still absent with the composite Brigade which had been sent against the Senussi, and the whole squadron which was with the composite regiment at Salonica, the Regiment once more found itself at full strength.

However, there was still much to be done before it could be considered even reasonably fit to again take the field. Of horses we had very few indeed, and these were the worst which had been left after they had been carefully picked over several times for the use of the above-mentioned expeditions. We were equally deficient in saddlery, clothing, and transport.

LACKING IN TRAINING

Furthermore, and this was the most important, a great deal of training was necessary. The draft from England proved to be of very good material ; perhaps on the young side, but nearly all willing. Their training, however, had left much to be desired, and they were very ignorant on many of the essential points.

I am in no way blaming the senior officers of the 2nd Regiment, as it was impossible for them to know the sort of training which would be most required, unless by close liaison with the 1st Line overseas ; and this, owing to the system at home of forming 2nd-Line Brigades under the command of a Brigadier, who had the final word as to the training to be given, was impossible.

Many of the N.C.O.'s, too, were a trouble at first, and there was a great deal too much of " we did this " or

" we did that at home " to allow the wheels of the new
machine to run as smoothly as one would have wished.

Another question of great difficulty was that of the
seniority of our old N.C.O.'s and that of those who had
been sent out from the 2nd Line. The same, incidentally, applied to the officers who had come out with them
and others who came out later.

THE RESOURCEFUL QUARTERMASTER

Major G. Strutt was appointed to command the
Regiment, having now returned from hospital, with
Major (then Captain) N. D'Arcy Clark as Second-in-Command, and Lieutenant Swanwick, who had also returned
from hospital, as Adjutant.

Amongst other old friends whom we were delighted
to meet again was R.S.M. Ward, who had not been
allowed to accompany the Regiment to Gallipoli.
Now, as always, his services became invaluable.

The first stage was to re-equip the Regiment, and
in this Lieutenant and Quartermaster J. Hodgson did
valuable work.

I do not know how it was worked, and indeed never
made too close enquiries, but this I do know, that
whilst other regiments were complaining that this and
that could not be procured, " Joey," as he was generally
known, invariably produced the article in question.

With the horses which we found still with the Regiment it was possible to mount only two or three troops,
but, as we soon began to draw remounts, this state of
things rapidly improved. Most of the remounts proved
to be either Australians or South Americans, some quite
good in appearance and many extremely bad, whilst
in all cases temper was an unknown quantity. The
one thing which one could feel fairly confident on was
the probability that hardly one of them had been
ridden more than a few times, if at all.

THE REMOUNTS—AND A BUCKJUMPER.

The days on which we drew remounts were always
days of great interest and heated argument. First of

all, officers wanted to select chargers, and this was done according to seniority. It was a common thing to hear two subalterns discussing the awful vice of some rather good-looking horse in a loud undertone, which was obviously meant to catch the ear of some senior officer standing by. The hope, which sometimes materialised, being that he would turn it down in consequence, and give the sub. an opportunity of annexing it as his own property.

When a bad batch of horses came in, it was astounding how squadron-leaders suddenly discovered that they were up to their establishment in horses, only to say in a few days' time that they were sorry to find that they had made a slight mistake, and that they were still short of ten.

Few horses, though, turned out to be really bad. One rather good Argentine turned out to be quite unmanageable. After giving him an honest trial, it was discovered one morning that he had broken his head-rope in the night, and could not be found. During the quiet of the same afternoon we were entertained by a most diverting display of buckjumping at the end of the horse lines of a neighbouring regiment. On the back of the refractory one had been strapped a machine-gun pack ; and ammunition boxes were flying in all directions.

Our search for the missing horse was pursued diligently, but, I fear, purposely in the wrong direction. Meanwhile, the attempts at horse-breaking continued daily, to our huge delight and satisfaction—for I have omitted to mention that we had witnessed the branding of the refractory one being carried out with great secrecy in the neighbouring lines previous to witnessing his first display.

What did it avail, therefore, when one morning a chit arrived from our neighbours to the effect that they believed that they had got one of our remounts " accidentally " mixed up with theirs ?

STRENGTHENING THE REGIMENT

On January 8th Major the Hon. D. Carleton, from the North Midland Mounted Brigade, was appointed as Second-in-Command, and on the following day we were strengthened by the arrival of Captain Rawlinson and Lieutenants Burdett, Humphries and Rogers from England, and also by the return of Major Shuttleworth from sick leave.

By this time the Regiment was finding its feet, and was inspected on the 12th by Major-General Peyton, being highly complimented by him.

We had been further strengthened also by the return of the officers and men who had been on the Senussi Expedition and, almost simultaneously with their arrival, heard that the whole Brigade, which was now nearly fully re-equipped, was to proceed to Salonica shortly.

Everyone in Mena camp envied us ; for although by now the whole of the 2nd Mounted Division had assembled there, only one other brigade had been mounted, and that had gone to the Canal.

It had already been decided that the Division was to be broken up for good and all. After working together for well over a year, everyone, from General Peyton downwards, felt this keenly.

I doubt if a finer body of men than those comprising the original Division had ever been put together. The men felt it, too, and in consequence a strong *esprit de corps* had grown up. Though sadly depleted by Gallipoli, the new drafts from home had turned out excellently, and there was every prospect of the Division being as good as it had ever been.

THE TROOPER'S SACK

To illustrate the keenness of some of these new men. A certain man left England, carrying, in addition to his kit, a small but heavy sack, the contents of which he kept a profound mystery. To all questions, he made the one answer : " You wait till we get to Egypt, and you'll wish you'd got it."

The sack survived the journey. Cairo was reached with the secret intact ; and also Mena Camp, with the desert of the Pharaohs around, fit setting for mystery. And here its bearer's face became a study.

" What is it, mate ? " asked someone.

" This ' ruddy ' sack," was the answer.

" Well, what's that to do with it ? "

" Why, it's full of sand to clean my bit with ! "

On January 19th the Regiment entrained at Cairo for Sidi Bishr, near Alexandria. It was the same arid place as when we first knew it in the previous April, only worse in every way, owing to the formation of many new and semi-permanent camps there. I know that we were extremely uncomfortable there, and that our arrival must have depressed us, for I see in the regimental diary this note: "Staff and camping arrangements bad, as usual."

The whole Brigade, under the command of Major, now Temporary Brigadier-General, F. Lance, was bivouacked close together, and training was proceeded with from the stage which we had reached when we left Cairo.

LIGHTER SIDE OF TRAINING

Even training sometimes had its light side. One day, when inspecting the Regiment, I had occasion to send the Adjutant with the following message : " The Colonel's compliments to Mr. B——, and will he hold his reins in the correct military way." Back came this answer : " Mr. B——'s compliments to the Colonel. He has always held his reins in his own way, and is too old to learn any other." Which, with all due respect to Mr. B., I really believe to have been the case.

On January 30th and 31st we were treated to a northerly gale, which, blowing unbroken from off the sea, raised a bad sand-storm, which not only succeeded in uprooting practically every tent, but in burying practically the whole of our kit and equipment, much of which went for good and all, for before we had time to straighten things up, we received orders that we were to embark for Salonica on February 2nd.

We were still short of a number of transport mules and limbers, but on the 31st we drew the latter from Ordnance, which was fortunate, as it was beginning to look as if we should have to leave nearly all we possessed behind us.

The night of the 1st was rather in the nature of a nightmare, being spent in packing limbers and trucks in pitch darkness, preparatory to marching at daybreak.

TROUBLES OF MOVING

Though such moves were common enough, no one will ever forget them ; the hurried dashing about at the last moment of men who had mislaid their sword, or rifle, in the darkness ; subalterns, with arms full of nosebags or picketing pegs, trying to find the culprits who would have left them ; limbers stuck axle deep in the sand, the missing horse, the inevitable saddle slipping round on the order to " mount," and the short-legged man who never could get on to his horse in full marching order !

All these and many others go to make up the miseries of a move in the dark, but, as on this occasion, everything had a knack of righting itself in the end, and by 9 a.m. on February 2nd we once more found ourselves afloat in Alexandria Harbour, this time on the S.S. *Minneapolis*, a fine ship of 12,000 tons, which was later on torpedoed and sunk.

After an uneventful, but circuitous, voyage, which was inevitable, owing to submarines, we found ourselves in Salonica harbour on the morning of the 7th.

CHAPTER IX

SALONICA—FROM THE SEA

APPROACHING Salonica from the sea, one's first impression is that it is a fair and goodly place. The harbour itself is a great expanse of water, flanked on the left as one enters it by flat, low-lying land, or rather swamps, and on the right by a long promontory of gently rising hills.

As one proceeds, the swamps give place to knolls, which become, in turn, foothills, leading up to a crescent of hills, perhaps 2,000 feet in height, facing the harbour on the north side. At the foot of these hills, and at the water's edge, is spread the long, white, straggling town of Salonica.

From the sea, and from that only, it is a fair spot. Rising sharply from the sea front, it is spread before one's vision, terrace after terrace of white, pink, and yellow houses, freely interspersed with the minarets of mosques without number ; whilst through the whole can be traced the ancient city walls, wandering away through the town and up the hill sides, where houses have ceased to be.

On landing, or rather on coming alongside the one and only quay, your first and most favourable impression is quickly and ruthlessly dispelled.

The quay itself is only capable of accommodating one ship at a time, and stands alongside a warehouse wrecked by bombs a few days previous to our arrival. Of facilities for loading and unloading there are none.

THE " CHOCOLATE SOLDIERS "

It was on this quay, on the occasion of our original landing on October 5th, that innumerable spies of

MAJOR G. WINTERBOTTOM

Commanded "A" Squadron, 1916, until killed in action, 1917

Germany, Bulgaria, Turkey, and Austria sat in rows, note-books in hand, busily jotting down every item of interest—our numbers, our equipment, and our units. Although at this date, February, 1916, this practice had openly ceased, it was still well and efficiently maintained, doubtless by the partisans of the King's party.

On landing, one's impressions became those of dirt, confusion, and narrow streets. If these were dispelled by the sight of picturesque gendarmerie in " Chocolate Soldier " uniforms, shiny black knee-boots, and long flowing knickerbockers of black silk, or by the sight of the old gateway from which St. Paul preached, it was for the moment only.

St. Paul makes mention of the rapacity of the Jews, and the number of the graves. Both of these are still much in evidence, and could have lost little in the intervening years.

As for the population, it appeared to represent every nationality under the sun, and several others besides. Spanish origin was apparent in many, and these, curiously enough, still talk the Spanish of the time of the Inquisition.

Of enthusiasm there was none, and could it be wondered at when one considered the political situation in the country ? Briefly, it was this.

We had made our first landing uninvited, and to suit our own interests or necessities. We found a country in two minds, each faction patriotic enough, but neither knowing in which direction their interests lay.

THE GREEK PARTIES

The King's party were superficially our friends, but secretly strongly pro-German, and intriguing night and day with that country for our undoing. The other party, headed by that splendid statesman and man, M. Venizelos, were equally pro-British, and anxious for an active entry into the war on our side. A third party existed, namely, the army, and of the politics and feelings of this we knew little.

H

To add to the complication, we were on neutral territory, and therefore, I suppose, liable to internment.

The Greek army was fully mobilised, and was stretched out along the Bulgarian frontier, some thirty-five miles north of Salonica, and into this zone our troops might not enter.

Our immediate necessity, therefore, was to put our base, Salonica, into a state of defence, so as to give our army a chance of withdrawal, should the worst happen. I shall refer to this presently.

A COMPLICATED SITUATION

The situation, therefore, was roughly as follows : The British army was concentrating round Salonica and its immediate neighbourhood, extending across the peninsular to Stavros, on the sea to the east. On the left of the British, and pushed up towards the Serbian frontier, was the French army, under General Sarreil.

Along the frontier lay a combined force of Germans, Austrians, Turks, and Bulgars, estimated at not less than 500,000, as against our combined total of not more than 100,000.

Between the British and the Bulgar frontier lay a tract of rough country, thirty miles in depth, and in this rested the Greek army of 400,000, which, though at the moment facing the Bulgars, might at any time turn round and combine with them against us.

Probably history has never shown a more complicated situation. Failing active hostilities against either us or the Bulgars, it seemed as if the Greeks, who were perfectly willing to fight something, would fight between themselves. This was our chief and only safeguard.

Before we can get on with the narrative, it will be best to give a brief description of the country.

At the head of the Gulf of Salonica lies the town and harbour of that name, and almost due east, thirty-five miles distant, is the head of the Gulf of Orfano and the small town of Stavros. Between the two runs a ridge of rough mountains, much broken up into spurs, which, passing Salonica seven miles to the north, terminates on the banks of the River Vardar, which has its exit to the sea a few miles west of that town.

NATURAL LINE OF DEFENCE

This line of mountains forms a natural line of defence to the town and harbour, and was forthwith selected by our army, under General Sir Bryan Mahon, for that purpose. This natural barrier became our line of concentration. Military roads were constructed up to it, guns from the fleet were placed in position behind the surrounding hills, which were, in turn, heavily entrenched and protected with barbed wire entanglements.

Between Salonica and Stavros lay the three-pronged promontory of Mount Athos, fifty miles in length, all of which was included in the British lines.

The River Vardar, at the west of Salonica, and in the zone of the French army, rises in the mountains of Serbia, and has a course almost due north and south passing through narrow valleys at the north, which gradually broaden out into a wide and flat one as the river approaches the sea.

At the east end of our lines, that is, at the head of the Gulf of Orfano, and a few miles east of Stavros, we find the River Struma, which finds its exit into the gulf by way of the brackish and muddy Sea of Tahinos.

For the last twenty miles of its course before reaching the sea the river runs N.W.-S.E. Here, at the Butkova Golu (lake), it turns nearly due east for twelve miles, flowing through a dead flat and most fertile plain, until we come to Demirhissar, a town at the foot of a high and rugged range of mountains, where it flows from its source in Bulgaria, through the narrow and almost precipitous pass of Rupel, the mouth of which is guarded by the Greek fort of that name.

THE FAMOUS STRUMA VALLEY

The triangle formed by this bend of the Struma river and the mountains to the north and south of it forms the famous Struma Valley, the most fertile part of all Greece, and probably one of the most fertile of the whole world. In width, it varies from seven to eighteen miles. The mountains to the north form the Bulgarian frontier.

Into Butkova Golu runs the Butkova river, which has a course practically due E. and W., running through a valley which forms a continuation of the Struma Valley itself, though narrower. At the head of this valley lies Lake Doiran, on the west end of which, nestling below the hills, rests the town of Doiran, which is Serbian, though practically on the frontier of that country, Greece, and Bulgaria.

Out of Lake Doiran runs the Kilindir River, which has a southerly course into Lake Ardzan, and thence into Lake Amatovo, and thence by the Azmac into the River Vardar, to which this chain of lakes runs almost parallel.

We thus roughly have a square, forty-five to fifty miles across; the south side formed by the French and British lines of defence, the west by the Vardar and the Serbian frontier, the north and east by the Struma Valley and its continuation, the Butkova valley, the mountains to the north of which form the Bulgarian frontier.

PRECIPITOUS MOUNTAINS

This frontier is literally a wall of almost precipitous mountains, rising to 6,000 feet, and pierced only by two passes of importance, one at Demirhissar, leading due north into Bulgaria, and one at the west end of Lake Doiran, running towards Strumnitza.

A few words as to the interior of this square, before we resume the narrative of the Regiment's doings.

After leaving the town of Salonica, the road will lead you over the shoulder of the hill, on the face of which the town rests, overlooking the harbour, after which you will come to a gently rising and undulating plateau, studded with numerous camps, all of which are of canvas, for as yet there has been no time, or material, with which to erect anything of a more permanent nature.

Passing through these, the road becomes steeper and more winding, until at length you will find yourself on the crest of the hills which form the natural defensive belt around, and nine miles beyond, the town.

THE DECEPTIVE PLAIN

Looking north from here, you will notice that the hills fall much more steeply than they do on the southern face. At the foot of them extends a dead flat plain, seven miles in width, studded here and there with villages, and, in the centre of it, the small town of Langaza. The plain looks, at first sight, to be extremely fertile, and so it would be but for the fact which you will quickly ascertain if you attempt to walk or ride across it, that it is little more than a bog. Across this plain stretches one road, which leads to Langaza, where it terminates near the foot of the hills bordering the north edge of the plain.

There is one other road to the west, though out of your sight, namely, the main road to the important town of Ceres, which is situated in the Struma Valley, a little east of Demirhissar. This road is the only communication between Salonica and the northern frontier.

Immediately to the east of Langaza, and in the centre of the plain, is the beautiful oval lake of the same name, beyond the far end of which, if it is clear, you may just see the end of the Besik Geul, a narrow lake of nearly twenty miles in length, extending almost due east nearly as far as Stavros, at the head of the Gulf of Orfano. The valley contracts as it nears the Besik Geul until the mountains on its northern shore run steeply down to the lake shore.

This group of mountains is called the Besik Dagh, and fills practically the whole of the area which I have already described, east and west from Stavros to the

Ceres-Salonica road, and north and south from the Langaza to the Struma Valley.

It was in this group of mountains that our lot was to be cast for the next two months.

POLICED BY A BRIGAND

The Besik Dagh group rises to some 4,000 feet in height, and is really a succession of gradually rising ridges, interspersed and much cut up with deep valleys and ravines between which are numerous plateaux, which in places are slightly cultivated. Along most of these valleys, and on all the plateaux, are numerous villages, of which more anon.

These are inhabited by every Macedonian race, for within the last twenty years the country has belonged to Turkey, Bulgaria, and Greece in turn.

It became the usual thing to find a village divided by what corresponds to the High Street into two very distinct parts. One side would be Turkish, and the other Greek, with a dash of Bulgar. The former may be distinguished by the cleanliness (comparatively speaking) of the houses and children, and the latter by the reverse.

No intercommunication between the two halves exists, law and order, also comparative, being usually enforced by a so-called Greek gendarme, who is usually a retired comitadji, *i.e.*, brigand of notoriety, and therefore commanding the respect, and, probably, the admiration, of both factions.

The custodian of Visoka, for instance, rejoiced in the name of Christos, which he most certainly belied, boasting, as he did, of something like fifteen murders, though he would not call them such. Christos was much mystified at my compass; it was the first he had ever seen, and he informed me that he had two aspirations : the first, a pair of English soldier's trousers ; the second, to tear a Bulgar's throat out with his teeth. Though able to accommodate him in the former respect, I was unable to supply the latter want.

A TRYING CHANGE OF CLIMATE

On February 7th the Regiment disembarked at Salonica. Every difficulty was encountered, owing to the cramped accommodation of the quay, and matters were made no better by an apparent total absence of any Staff work. Almost immediately after disembarking, R.S.M. Ward, much to our regret, had an accident to his knee, and had to go to hospital, and eventually home—a serious loss to the Regiment.

After disembarking, the Regiment was marched to Akbuna Camp, seven miles north-west of Salonica, and there went into bivouac. It was a poor spot at the best of times, being open and exposed to every wind, and, believe me, at this time of the year, winds were cold to a degree.

This did not matter so much, but what really did worry us was the bad water for our horses. The quantity was sufficient, but the quality bad, owing, we thought, to pollution from the camps higher up. Whatever the cause, our horses absolutely refused to drink, and within four days had lost all the condition which they had put on in Egypt. Apart from this, the change of climate was most trying to men and horses alike.

One of the most noticeable things of the war was, to my mind, the extraordinary rapidity with which horses and mules adapted themselves to rapid changes of climate, and the rapidity with which, on being moved from a hot to a cold climate, they would grow their coats.

During the first few days at Akbuna we had sharp frosts at night, and, in consequence, a series of hospital cases, owing to falls, the horses, after their long spell in Egypt, being quite unused to slippery surfaces. Up to the 12th we had seventeen men sent to hospital, but not all owing to the above cause.

THE FIRST BLIZZARD

On the 12th and 13th we experienced our first blizzard ; torrents of rain in the camp, and heavy snow on the hills, together with an icy cold wind. Men and horses were half frozen. So cold was it that even the sheepskins, with which we were provided, placed over our overcoats, and every other particle of clothing which we could cram on, in no wise added to our comfort. The camp became a sea of cold mud, but, fortunately, a cold drying wind helped to rectify this.

On February 14th I see the following entry in the diary :—

> 14th, nil, except that the Quartermaster was detected in the act of annexing four mules belonging to another unit. As a rule, his attempts at petty and greater larceny have been attended with success, to the great advantage of the Regiment.

On the 16th the Regiment marched to Langaza, which I have already mentioned, and bivouacked on the bank of the Langaza river—a shallow, quick-flowing stream, which showed great persistency in endeavouring to flood out the camp after each successive rainfall.

Having drawn mules to complete establishment on the 13th, considerable delay was caused in getting under way on the morning of the move. Those, and those only, who have had to contend with new mules, heavily loaded limbers, new harness, deep mud and darkness, will be able to sympathise with a transport officer on such an occasion.

Up till the 21st the weather had changed for the better, and there was a feel of spring in the air—the springs being very early in Macedonia, but on that day and the following it became bitterly cold ; the water freezing in tents even when they contained braziers. On the 21st " B " Squadron, under Major Shuttleworth, moved to Langavuk, at the east end of Lake Langaza, and " D " Squadron, under Captain N. D'Arcy Clark, to Stavros. " A " Squadron, under Captain Rawlinson, remained at Langaza with Headquarters.

ATTACK BY BULGARS

On the following day the men of the Derbyshire Squadron of the composite regiment which had landed in Salonica on October 10th rejoined their respective squadrons, so that the Regiment was once more, after many months, united and up to establishment.

This squadron had for some time been at Langavuk under the command of Captain R. Birchenough, with Lieutenant Buckston as second-in-command. Since their landing in October they had had a hard time.

On October 5th the 10th Division had been landed from Gallipoli, and within a few days had been pushed up to Lake Doiran and rather beyond. The Derbyshire and, I think, the Sherwood Squadrons accompanied them, and provided the day outpost line until the memorable attack by the Bulgars one cold, misty night.

This attack was completely successful. Our casualties amongst the infantry were very heavy, and the remainder had to seek safety in a hurried retirement to Salonica, suffering intensely from the cold and frost-bite, having lost all their heavy clothing.

During this retirement the Yeomanry formed the rear-guard, and did what was possible to delay the advance of the enemy until the rear of the infantry had got clear of Doiran and its surroundings.

For a time the Bulgars were in possession of one end of Doiran town, whilst the Yeomanry were in possession of the other.

During the ensuing winter they were occupied in patrolling amongst the hills to the north of Salonica, and had a very hard time in consequence, as this duty necessitated their being bivouacked at a considerable altitude, and, for the most part, without tents.

The horses, however, stood it well, and very few were lost, though, as was to be expected, their condition was very poor when they once more rejoined the Regiment. It is a wonder that they survived at all, as, in addition to the cold, there was a great lack of forage. So used had some of the men become to sleeping out in the cold that, on rejoining their proper squadrons, I heard of several cases of men refusing to sleep in tents, now that they had the opportunity.

PATROLLED THE WHOLE FRONT

The reason for this wide dispersal of the squadrons was that the Brigade had been given the task of patrolling and reconnoitring the whole of the British front, whilst the infantry and engineers were hard at work constructing and fortifying the hills round Salonica.

They had a very heavy task in front of them, and the length of time at their disposal was an uncertain quantity, as every day fresh rumours filtered through, indicating the possibility of an early attack in great force on the part of the enemy, with the laudable intention of driving us into the sea.

I do not know the actual width of the zone which the Brigade was responsible for, but it must have been well over a hundred miles, as the area allotted to the Derbyshires covered a front of sixty-five miles. In addition to the constant patrolling of this line, our orders were to patrol forward to a depth not exceeding twenty-five miles. I say " not exceeding " because at that distance north the area occupied by the Greek army commenced, and it was certain that they would resent any such intrusion if carried out systematically.

To cover this front it was absolutely essential that the squadrons should be widely separated. Stavros, which was the Headquarters of " D " Squadron, was forty-five miles east of Langaza, whilst " B " Squadron at Langavuk was about eighteen miles east of the same place.

Owing to the mountainous and exceedingly rough nature of the country ahead of us, and the total absence of roads, it was obviously impossible for a patrol to reach its twenty-five-mile limit and to return to camp the same night. It therefore became necessary for each squadron to send out a detached troop as far forward as the squadron could ration them, which usually meant to the foot of the mountains, and for this troop to bivouac out for three days at a time, during which time it found all the patrols in the sector of that squadron by day, and served as a picket over its squadron by night.

The patrols of each squadron were arranged so as to overlap the sectors of the squadrons to right and left of it, so as to give different patrols the chance of meeting and establishing communication. This intercommunication was well maintained, and I frequently received messages at Langaza detailing the work which had been done at Stavros two days previously.

THE AUSTRIAN MAP MAKER

The very first day that the patrols went out was sufficient to show us that the maps in our possession, which, by the way, were Austrian ones, were entirely wrong. Practically every patrol which had been given a definite point to make for returned without having been able to find it. It is true that a few villages shown on the map were located, but in nearly every case these were several miles away from where they should have been.

It eventually transpired that the Austrian who had compiled the map had done so whilst staying comfortably at Stavros, whence it was reported that he had made rather a hobby of sampling the numerous Greek wines, and that his method had been to get any stray shepherd who happened along to point out with his finger on the unfilled map sheet where he had come from, and the name of his village. This explained most things, but not everything.

Time after time a patrol going to a village would locate one more or less where expected, but on enquiry, a name would be given totally different from that shown, whilst another patrol, miles away, would unexpectedly come across the identical village for which the first patrol had been searching.

Everyone nowadays is so accustomed to map reading, and working to a map which is accurate and which can be relied on to bring you to where you want to go, that the first time one comes on an inaccurate one, without knowing it, and consequently fetches up at some totally different place to which one had expected, one is overcome with a sense of utter bewilderment.

There being no roads, and only a few very rough sheep-tracks, one is at first naturally inclined to blame oneself, or someone else in preference. The real reason for towns and villages being where they should not be was not far to seek.

VILLAGES OUT OF PLACE

Within the past fifteen years the whole of Macedonia had been fought over time and again, and had in turn been Turkish, Bulgar, and Greek. In each war both sides had done their level best not only to massacre the local inhabitants, but to entirely destroy their villages. Thus a few survivors from a Bulgar village might settle down, miles away, on the site of a devastated Turkish hamlet, and, there being no inhabitants there, would naturally christen it with the name of their late home.

Those, on the other hand, who had escaped from the Turkish village might equally well give its name to the site of what had once been a Greek village. Thus it was quite possible for one and the same place to have three different names according to the nationality of the individual who volunteered you the information.

Not only so, the map might show one village, say Janis, but on going to seek it you would discover no less than six villages, and not one of them of that name. This was accounted for by the fact that Janis was the name of what might correspond roughly to an urban district council area.

Many flourishing villages were shown on the map where nothing existed at all. In most of these cases it was discovered that the name belonged to a pre-historic town, possibly of the time of Alexander of Macedon, and had been handed down from mouth to mouth throughout the centuries.

It will be readily understood that we not only quickly

gave up trying to find our way by our maps, but advised the army authorities to do the same.

LEARNING TO MAKE MAPS

As was only to be expected, we promptly received orders to make maps. This was a very different proposition to following up mountain tracks to find where they led to, or trying to ascertain the correct name of a village. It would be, of course, simple enough to jot down the course of the former, providing one only knew exactly where one really had started from, and where one had finished.

Map making was almost an unknown art to the Regiment, although Lieutenant Hayward was credited with great knowledge on the subject. Lieutenant Hayward was, however, at Stavros and could not be spared. A ray of light appeared when Major Carleton pronounced that "map makers always did it by triangulation."

Starting with Langaza Lake, the position and length of which we accepted as being fairly accurate, we succeeded in fixing the position of the top of a fairly high hill, which could be easily distinguished from others. From what purported to be accurate compass bearings, this hill appeared to have been in about a dozen different places at one and the same time, but by taking the mean of these I believe the ultimate position allotted to it was not far wrong.

All patrols were ordered to take all the bearings they could whilst out on patrol, and masses of data and sketches soon began to pour in, which it became my self-appointed task to plot on the map.

Some of the mountains must have been full of iron-stone, which gave great deviation in the compass readings, and this made plotting a difficult matter. For instance, bearings taken to the small town of Visoka from the south-west gave it a totally different position from that arrived at from others taken from the south-east.

The result, however, appeared to give satisfaction, and was utilised for some time by both our own army and the French. If not actually accurate, a stranger could at least arrive at the right village, which was more than could be said for the Austrian production.

DOCTOR'S PESSIMISTIC REPORT

Another order given to the Brigade was to make a census of our area—not a mere census, showing the number of inhabitants, but a regular encyclopedia, giving the names of the headmen of the villages, the number of sheep, hens and pigs, and the amount of available forage.

As the last was nearly always hidden in the roofs of the houses, on purpose to escape our notice, and as the sheep were always out grazing in most inaccessible places, usually without any shepherd, and guarded by a number of huge and extremely fierce dogs, the collection of detail became a matter of some difficulty.

Captain M. Wilson, our regimental doctor, who had come to Salonica with the composite regiment in October, meanwhile carried out his own special reconnaissances—in his case, testing water and examining children for malaria.

His reports did not inspire us with hope for the future, as they went to show that practically every individual was rotten with it, and that it appeared to be of several types, all of which were much more virulent than anything we could meet elsewhere. As events proved, no one ever spoke a truer word of warning.

I think we were all rather taken aback when informed that the " pot-bellies " we had noticed on the small infants (who usually ran about naked, or nearly so) were not to be ascribed to good feeding, as we had fondly imagined, but to enlarged spleens, the result of malaria.

When we advanced further up country the " pot-bellies " were even more in evidence, though their owners were in many cases on the verge of starvation.

INQUIRIES AS TO GREEK ARMY

During this period two special officers' patrols were carried out for G.H.Q. As the object of both these was to glean information about the Greek army and its doings, and as the said army by no means welcomed Allied officers who might be prying around, especially after the blowing-up of the Demirhissar bridge by the French, the success of the patrols had largely to depend on guile and an innocent exterior.

Lieutenant Hayward was selected for the first of these, and was given an extremely difficult task to perform, namely, to report in full on the construction, etc., of all the Greek bridges in the Ceres area. This report, moreover, was wanted by G.H.Q. within a week.

Lieutenant Hayward, by profession an architect, was the very man for the job, and made a great success of it, and was complimented by G.H.Q.

A CLEVER RUSE

To reach G.H.Q. within the specified time he had to ride eighty miles in the last twenty-four hours, and this over mountains totally devoid of roads, and in the winter.

To reach the Greek zone he had to take pack animals, carrying forage for his outgoing and return journey. Having sent these back before reaching his destination, he arrived amongst the Greeks as a hungry wanderer who had lost his way, and craved their hospitality, which was readily given.

To satisfy the Greek authorities, he was taken to their Headquarters at Ceres, over the very bridges which he wished to reconnoitre. Thanks to a skilled eye, a good memory, and knowing the length of his horse's stride, he was able to produce, when once clear of the Greeks, a detailed drawing, practically to scale, of something like six bridges.

The second patrol, under Captain Rawlinson, was entirely to find out the general feeling in the Greek army, and also as much as possible as to their dispositions.

This patrol was also a success. Practically the same *modus operandi* was adopted, and in this case Captain Rawlinson succeeded in ingratiating himself into the affections of a Greek Divisional General and his Staff ; remaining as their guest for some days.

He seems to have won their confidence by his ability to consume and to carry more wine than the whole Staff put together, and also by beating the General in a revolver match !

He carried with him a wire-tapper, an instrument apparently unknown to the Greeks, and gave his hosts demonstrations with it, thus tapping a number of messages under their noses—but, unfortunately, I believe, none of these were of much import.

With the beginning of March spring came with a rush, and with it came glorious weather. In Macedonia there is none of the gradual approach of spring to which we are accustomed in England. There it is on you before you know what has happened, and within the space of a fortnight the hill-tops become a mass of crocus—white, purple and yellow—whilst in the plains flowers of every description begin to make their appearance.

Later on, in early May, the country becomes a gardener's paradise. But to the average individual the chief impression left is of acres upon acres of pink and white asphodels on the hill-tops, and fields upon fields of gorgeous poppies—white, red and dark purple. These are one of the staple crops in Macedonia, and are of great height and size.

GAME PLENTIFUL

I doubt if there is a more naturally fertile country in the world, and taken properly in hand its possibilities are immense.

As you ride across the plains you will come on deep narrow crevasses in the soil, caused by the sudden terrific rains and waterspouts of the early summer, and here you will see nothing but the richest of soil, with

MAJOR R. P. BIRCHENOUGH

Commanded " A " Squadron, 1918 until 1919

never a stone or pebble in it, reaching down to a depth
of thirty feet.

Not only is the land fertile in the extreme, but the
mountains are equally rich in minerals—coal, lead,
copper and iron, as well as talc, seem all to be there.

There are also many springs of mineral properties,
and at Langaza we were singularly fortunate ; for
within a mile of the town still stood a Roman bath,
the basin built of marble, into which flowed a hot
spring of clear water. The water was full of sulphur,
and just not too hot to be unpleasant.

Game, too, there was in abundance. On the lakes
enormous flocks of duck of every variety, and wild
geese by many thousands. The margins of the lakes
literally swarmed with snipe, whilst on the foot-hills
were quantities of partridges, with a good sprinkling
of brown hares. At Stavros there were many woodcock
and a few pheasants.

How all this game survived is a mystery, as in no
other country are there such quantities of hawks,
eagles and harriers apparently of every known variety.
Fortunately, we had at least two guns in the Regiment,
so that the larder was seldom without game. The
partridges appear to pair much later in Salonica than
in England.

Whilst talking of the birds, mention must be made of
a flock of pelicans which arrived at Langaza Lake
towards the end of February, apparently with the
intention of nesting there. Everyone, too, will remember the dear old storks, who arrived soon afterwards
and built huge nests on almost every chimney top.

The lakes swarmed with coarse fish, but, unfortunately,
tackle was to all intents and purposes absent.

FROG FISHING

Everyone will recall the frogs which, in their countless
millions, made night a perfect uproar, and on several
occasions made one believe that there was a Zeppelin
low overhead. However, as these frogs turned out

I

to be of the edible sort and were, moreover, of great size, their sins were forgiven them.

At one time, frog fishing, after work was done, became quite a rage. The method favoured was a rod which would reach well over a pool, a bent pin and a shred of bully-beef, for which a frog would literally leap out of the water. Their thighs, fried on a piece of toast with a bit of bacon, were excellent.

Other disturbers of the night were the Balkan sheep-dogs, which resemble overgrown timber wolves more than anything else. These, at Langaza, used to make nightly descents on the cook-house, and would even force their way into the officers' mess tent.

Our regimental Cook-Sergeant one night made a wonderful shot at one of these, killing it stone dead with a single shot from a ·22 bore rifle. This dog measured six feet from the nose to the tip of his tail. Incidentally, these Balkan sheep-dogs are exceedingly fierce, and several cases occurred of men of the Salonica force being killed and partially eaten by them.

CHAPTER X

SALONICA—*continued*

PICTURESQUE INHABITANTS, BUT —

THE inhabitants, whom I seem to have forgotten, were extremely picturesque and equally dirty. Their morals, I am told, were on a par with their cleanliness.

The costumes worn were innumerable, and varied from the baggy blue trousers and broad red comurbund of the Turks, to the rough grey homespun kilt worn over tight-fitting trousers and puttees of the highland Greeks. They mostly appeared to be friendly, but could not be trusted a yard, and it was never safe for any British Tommy, or " Johnnie," as the Greeks called them, to go alone.

There were numerous cases of British soldiers being murdered, and it was known that a number of Bulgar comitadjis (brigands) who had sworn undying hatred against us were going about disguised as peaceful Greek shepherds, sheep and all complete, merely waiting the chance of catching a British soldier, alone and off his guard, to put a knife into him.

For the most part, the Turks seemed apathetic about the war, and were firmly convinced that they would win, as they had the support of the Kaiser, whom they had been told from Constantinople was a reincarnation of Mahommed. " It is useless to fight against God " was their general tone.

Of all the inhabitants of Macedonia, the Turks were the most reliable, as well as the cleanest. If a Turk gave you his hospitality, even though his nation was at war with yours, you would be perfectly safe. If a patrol had to stay out a night at any village, it almost invariably selected the best-looking Turkish house, and was as invariably shown the best of hospitality under the existing circumstances.

Having dealt briefly with dogs, game, flowers, frogs, fish, and the inhabitants, we had better get on with the book, which was by way of being a war history of the Regiment, and not a Baedeker.

AN AERIAL BATTLE

On March 24th the Regiment received orders to move, and accordingly left Langaza on the 25th. That is, "A" and "B" Squadrons left, as "D" Squadron were to follow from Stavros independently.

This move included the whole Brigade; which, after a long march, camped for the night at the Semetli Drift. Though we did not know our ultimate destination, our direction was north-west, and this we knew would put us clear of the left flank of the Greek army.

All tents were left behind, and bivouac sheets were issued and used for the first time. These sheets were 7 feet by 4 feet, and two, buttoned together, made a tent just big enough for two men to lie down in. Each man was issued with one sheet, and each officer with two.

Our tents were left standing at Langaza, and a few hours after our departure a German aeroplane flew over and bombed the empty camp; dropping one bomb immediately outside the orderly room tent.

No incident occurred on this march excepting the loss of the headquarters cookery book!

The march was resumed the following day, until reaching Kukus, some forty-five miles north-west of Langaza. Here orders were given to the Regiment to go into camp in the bed of the Spant river, two miles north-east of Kukus. The South Notts went into camp on the opposite bank to us, and the Sherwoods several miles further to the east.

On the 27th we witnessed our first aerial battle on a large scale. It appeared that the Germans had conducted an air raid on Salonica, and during their retirement were caught by the French just as they reached Kukus. We saw three machines brought down in as many minutes, and though it was officially reported that they were German ones we all had grave doubts on the matter.

On the 29th the Sherwoods and South Notts were moved six miles to our north-west, where they immediately got in touch with the enemy.

A NIGHT ALARM

The Derbyshires were left at Spant river in support, and special precautions were adopted, as nothing was known of the enemy except that they were reasonably near—some considerable bodies of comitadjis were reported by the French to be in the neighbourhood. We were now on the extreme left flank of the British zone, and forming a liaison with the French, who had a Brigade of Chasseurs d'Afrique on our immediate left.

On April 1st Lieutenant G. Winterbottom arrived at Salonica, with a few men as reinforcements. This was a pouring wet day, but the men by now had learned to look after themselves when in bivouac, and were none the worse.

The previous fortnight had been gloriously fine and quite hot, with the result that the young grass had come up well, and our horses were already beginning to show a marked improvement in condition. The cold and wet of the early spring, coupled with the heavy patrol work, had pulled them down considerably. Taking all in all, it was wonderful how well they had stood it, and even more so how extraordinarily active and sure-footed they had become. It was quite common to take a troop where no self-respecting Scotch hill pony would have dreamed of going in pre-war days.

German aeroplanes came over most days about now, and though they usually dropped a bomb or two round about Kukus, they never molested us. On April 2nd there was heavy artillery fire in the direction of Lake Doiran, and on the 4th the Regiment received the alarm at 3 a.m. This meant an immediate packing up of the whole camp, and the loading of the transport in the dark. This was accomplished, and the Regiment was ready to move off, complete in every detail, in one-and-a-half hours, no bad performance for the first night alarm.

On the 7th orders were received to move to Janis (nine miles further east), in order to fill in a gap which existed between the Sherwoods and the Chasseurs d'Afrique, but at midnight the order was cancelled from England! As this move was counter-ordered, " A " Squadron were sent up to reinforce the Sherwoods at Irikli.

NATURAL SODA-WATER

On the 8th the Regiment was inspected by General Sir Bryan Mahon, the Commander-in-Chief, and the same afternoon one troop was sent to Kilindir. Kilindir is the last station on the railway to the town of Doiran, and lay just within our advanced outpost line, and between the right of the Chasseurs, whose headquarters were at Hirsova, and the left of the Sherwoods, who were guarding the Gola Ridge by a chain of outposts, their headquarters, as I have said, being at Irikli, six miles south-west of Kilindir.

Major Carleton having gone on leave, Major Shuttleworth was appointed Second-in-Command in his place, and Captain Rawlinson was transferred from " A " Squadron to " B " Squadron.

On the 13th orders again came for a move, and this was carried out the following day, when we went into camp at Hadji-Janis, half way between Janis and Hirsova, where the French were, and six miles south of Kilindir.

There is nothing worthy of mention about Hadji-Janis, which is merely a name on the map, except that on the hill-top above the camp were the remains of a large castle, or fortified camp, which must have been of extreme antiquity.

As in many places, we were very short of water for

our horses, but this was somewhat compensated for by an ancient well a mile from camp. This was a mineral well, and equal in quality to Salutaris. It was, indeed, a novelty, to say nothing of being a pleasure, to draw up soda-water by the bucket. Unfortunately, or possibly fortunately, the horses would not look at it.

For some unaccountable reason, the men for a time shared the distrust of the horses, maintaining that it contained arsenic!

As it was found that this camp was too far away for the support of our outpost at Kilindir, we moved the Regiment on the 16th to a point one mile south of Hirsova, and one-and-a-half miles south of Kilindir. Here we found good water running through a narrow and twisting nullah, in the bottom of which we pitched our camp.

To conform with the ground, the camp was long and straggling, and as it was sheltered by steep banks on each side, this was most desirable, as to be out on the flat plain was to court trouble from aeroplanes, whose attentions were daily becoming more marked.

As the Regiment, at one time and another, had a good deal to do with the Gola Ridge, it will be as well, perhaps, to give a rough description of the country before we continue.

THE MOUNTAINOUS COUNTRY

If in an aeroplane, you would see Salonica, with its semi-circle of hills, parallel to which, and to the north, the Langaza valley with a massif of rough hills beyond it falling, after twenty-five miles, into the broad, flat plain of the Struma Valley.

Thirty miles to the left, *i.e.*, the west of the head of the Langaza valley, and separated from it by a series of rough foothills, you would see another plain extending due north, that is, at right angles to that of Langaza. On the right, or east, this plain is flanked by a ridge of rough mountains stretching for ten miles due north and then suddenly terminating.

Looking towards the left, or west, the plain stretches for many miles, broken here and there by low hills. You would see the lakes which I have previously mentioned, Amatovo and Ochrida, and still further west the River Vardar, hemmed in to the west by a chain of almost precipitous mountains, rising to a height of six or seven thousand feet.

Looking half-left, that is, roughly north-west, you would see more mountains bordering the north edge of the plain, which is here about ten miles in depth. These mountains, commencing as mere hillocks on the edge of the plain, rise in a series of waves, culminating in a big, round-topped fellow of four or five thousand feet.

These mountains were held by the Germans and Bulgars, and immediately behind them was the town of Doiran, resting on the west end of the lake of that name.

THE GOLA RIDGE

These hills run at right angles to those I have mentioned as bordering the east of the plain, but between them there is a gap of six miles. This gap is called the Gola Ridge, which forms, so to speak, the northern lip of the plain, or, I should say, plateau, for beyond this the ground falls gradually away till it reaches the shore of Lake Doiran and the wide plain to the east of it, which I have already mentioned as forming a continuation of the Struma Valley.

This ridge constituted the advanced outpost line held by our Brigade, which line was continued to our left by the Chasseurs amongst the lower hills of the mountains guarding Doiran.

Kilindir lies on the banks of the river of that name which flows south from Lake Doiran through a typically Scottish glen, separating the west end of the Gola Ridge from the right of the mountains guarding Doiran town.

Having taken a bird's-eye look of the general lie of the land, let us have a more detailed look towards the German or Bulgar lines from the Gola Ridge itself.

As you reach the northern edge of the ridge you will get a glorious view. The ground falls gradually away from where you are standing until it reaches the shores of Lake Doiran, two miles away.

TOWARDS THE BULGAR LINES

This ground, on its higher slopes, is much cut up by deep, narrow gullies, which open out and eventually disappear as the slope levels out ; here the ground is covered with scrub and tall crops of maize, six to seven feet, or more, in height.

Half way down this slope, and immediately in front of one, nestles, in a clump of tall trees, the deserted hamlet of Patros.

I must qualify the word " deserted " as it proved to be occupied by two Greek policemen, of whom more later.

Two miles to our right, and a mile below the crest of the ridge, we could see another village, or, rather, small town, by name Sirlovo, and immediately above it, on the crest itself, the village of Gola. Both the latter were inhabited, and their inhabitants, being Bulgars for the most part, were no friends of ours.

Looking to the left, we could see the line of the Kilindir river, which runs through the glen which I have already mentioned as being on the extreme left, and, of course, below the ridge. Beyond the river, and parallel to it, runs a ridge of hills which drop steeply down to the lake shore, at which point we could see Doiran station.

This ridge of hills was occupied by the enemy, and with the mountains facing the French, and covering the approach to the town from the south formed, as it were, the short leg of the letter " L," Doiran town being in the angle formed by the two legs.

The lake is almost circular and about six miles in length, its eastern end being almost opposite the corresponding end of the Gola Ridge. Between Patros and the lake is a thick wood, about one-and-a-half miles long.

Extending the whole length of our view, and three miles beyond the lake, rose almost precipitously to a height of 5,000 feet the mountains of the Belashitza range. This range is the natural rampart of Bulgaria, and extends from the west end of Lake Doiran, where one can just see the road and pass leading from Doiran town to Strumnitza, right along the northern edge of the Struma Valley until it meets the sea. In all this length there is only one road and pass piercing its heights, namely, that at Demirhissar, the exit to which on the Greek side is guarded by Fort Rupel, a modern fortress of great strength.

In the centre of the plain, and almost on the eastern end of the lake, lies the small town of Brest, which was occupied by the enemy. Between us and the edge of the lake was all " No Man's Land."

It was shortly after our arrival on the Gola Ridge that the Greeks, presumably at the instigation of their King, retired from Fort Rupel, handing it over intact to the Bulgars, who thus secured a direct entry into the plain of the Struma Valley. This shortly afterwards necessitated the extension of the British front along the line hitherto occupied by the Greek army.

FRENCH SPOIL A CAPTURE

In the early days on the ridge, and before the Derby-shires had been moved up to it, it was an almost everyday occurrence for the Sherwoods to see patrols of Uhlans passing from Doiran to Brest, or to meet them recon-noitring up to Gola (on the top of the ridge) and beyond. At this stage, several patrol encounters took place, but by the time that we were moved up the enemy had learnt discretion, and were by no means easily met with.

A few days after we took over the Kilindir post we had a good opportunity, which was entirely spoilt by the French, of bagging a patrol of forty Uhlans.

This patrol had been seen moving up the road from Doiran station to Kilindir, with only one advanced point out ahead. They were advancing beautifully into the trap which was being formed by moving two troops behind the hills on their flank, so as to get well behind their only line of retreat.   Unfortunately, when another five minutes would have completed the movement, a French outpost must needs open fire at 900 yards on the single advanced scout, thus spoiling the whole thing.

Half an hour later, when the Uhlans were half way back to Doiran, a troop of Chasseurs from Hirsova came galloping past Kilindir, their swords drawn and the tails of their white Arab ponies streaming in the wind, and shouting at the top of their voices : " Ou sont les Boches ?   Ou sont les Boches ? " disappeared from view.

The same sort of thing happened to other regiments of the Brigade.   The Chasseurs were gallant enough, too much so for patrol fighting, but that was no use against the wily Uhlan, who required taking unawares, if at all.

UHLANS NEARLY BAGGED

A few days later, on the 17th, two troops of " A " Squadron co-operated with the Sherwoods in trying to round up a large patrol which had been seen for several days at dawn.   On this occasion, no less than three squadrons of Uhlans put in an appearance, and came along just as we would have wished.   All looked well for a big bag, and then the usual disappointment came.   The Sherwoods' machine-guns opened fire at 400 yards, and after firing a few rounds both jammed. The Uhlans retired till they reached a covering force of their own infantry at Doiran station, and were pursued by the Sherwoods up to that point, but the main body escaped with only a few casualties.   One of these, we were subsequently informed by the Greek policeman at Patros, was their sergeant-major, who was mortally wounded.   We had daily bulletins as to his progress, or otherwise, from the same source of information until the fourth day, when he was reported dead.

On the 18th the Regiment took over the whole of the ridge, whilst the Sherwoods and South Notts went into support and reserve. The method adopted by the Brigade was to maintain a day outpost line on the ridge, and from these outposts patrols were sent down into the plain. These outposts were withdrawn at night, and a line of strong pickets formed about a mile further back.

UHLAN PATROLS' FAVOURITE PLAN

Within the previous week the Chasseurs had twice been ambushed at dawn by Uhlans, who had occupied their day outpost line as soon as the Chasseurs had left it at dusk, and had awaited their arrival the following morning. I therefore decided to leave out a small post at night on our day outpost line, connected by telephone with the squadron at Kilindir.

It was lucky this was done, as on the very first night on which it was tried brother Boche came along to the tune of a troop of Uhlans, supported by about thirty infantry, evidently intent on playing the same game on us.

Our post got clear by the skin of their teeth, and had an exciting night gallop, with the Uhlans on their heels. The purpose was served, however, and the Boche gave up this plan for the future.

A favourite plan of the Uhlan patrols, who, incidentally, were mounted on excellent horses, Irish bred apparently, was to ride out until our patrols showed themselves, and then to gallop away and try to decoy the pursuing patrol on to infantry and machine-guns who had remained hidden. This plan never met with any success, as the Chasseurs had already been caught that way, and had "made us wise."

Taking it all round, the Uhlans never showed much initiative, and no ingenuity, and this gradually got less and less, until it was safe for our patrols to go unmolested right to the shores of Doiran itself.

A VILLAGE OF SPIES

The situation on the ridge was somewhat unique. The village of Gola was occupied by Bulgars, but on Greek territory, and as this was nominally neutral we had no power to turn them out. It goes without saying that they were spies to a man, and there is little doubt that, after we had withdrawn our outposts at night, and this had to be done for tactical reasons, the Boche came up and received all the information which the Gola inhabitants had collected during the day.

We always supposed that they had a system of signalling to the enemy by day, namely, to hang out washing of different colours to signify our presence, or otherwise. This form of signalling was almost impossible to prove and, moreover, could be carried out in broad daylight and read, by means of telescopes, by the enemy at a great distance.

I have already mentioned the village of Patros on the lower slopes as being inhabited by two policemen. This village was a favourite place of call, at first, for hostile patrols. It eventually transpired that one policeman was pro-German and the other pro-British. Either of these could pass as they pleased through either of the two opposing lines.

One day the pro-British policeman came and saw me on the ridge, and made an arrangement whereby he was to notify the presence of enemy patrols in the village. This arrangement was simple, and consisted of hanging out his shirt, which was black, from the back window, which faced the ridge, in the case of a patrol being present, and to refrain from doing so if one was not. Though I believe he was honest, Patros was nevertheless always approached with every precaution.

On April 19th the Regiment (" A " Squadron) carried out a good patrol to investigate the Doiran—Akinzali railway. Doiran station was almost reached, and the bridge there found to have been destroyed, whilst on the right patrols pushed right through the wood below

Patros, which up till then had always been reputed to contain a permanent force of German infantry and machine-guns, and on beyond it till they reached the shores of the lake.

On the same day the first of our infantry (1st Brigade) arrived, and a battalion of Manchesters, with whom we were ordered to co-operate, bivouacked on the open plain, contrary to advice, immediately in front of us and a mile south of Hirsova.

AIRCRAFT BROUGHT DOWN

The same afternoon Lieutenant Gillett tried an ingenious mounting for his machine-guns of his own contriving. This mounting was for anti-aircraft purposes, and was formed by tipping over a G.S. limber wagon on to its side. A gun was then clamped on to the upper wheel, and with the gunner sitting on the pole of the limber, the whole contrivance was free to turn in a complete circle, being pivoted on the wheel which lay on the ground.

The firing in itself was completely successful, but one fatality marred the experiment, for Lieutenant Swanwick's (Adjutant) pony " Micky," a general pet, was startled by the firing and fell over a low cliff, breaking his neck.

April 21st was Good Friday, and as the Padre could not come to us on Easter Day, it was decided to hold our Easter Day service on the 21st instead. Whilst communion service was in progress, a Boche 'plane chose the opportunity to visit us. Flying at a low altitude, he dropped three bombs whilst we were kneeling to receive the Sacrament, but these, I am glad to say, all fell in the Manchesters' camp.

Gillett promptly got on to the Boche with his machine-guns a few yards away from the extemporised communion table, and though the service continued without interruption, I am afraid that our minds were not filled with the thoughts with which they should have been.

We all thought that we saw the 'plane give an unusual swerve—certainly he changed his course, and flew out of sight over some low hills and into the French zone, and it was not until several days later that we heard that he had come down, hit, in their lines.

On the following day orders were received that the outpost line was to be withdrawn further back, and that the Regiment was to retire and go into camp near Janis on the next day, the 24th.

THE " NUNC DIMITTIS " !

At 10.30 that night a rather excited message came from the Manchesters saying that the French had telephoned from Hirsova that the Bulgars were massing, and looked as if they were about to try a *coup de main*, and with it came an order to pack and prepare to move. As our outpost at Kilindir had nothing to report, we took no notice and stayed comfortably in bed.

In a short while, however, a further and more peremptory order came, and as we had been told to conform with the infantry, there was nothing left for it but to comply. Much against our will we commenced to pack, and all was ready to move after two hours, but as no orders to do so arrived, there we stayed, cursing both inwardly and openly until daylight came.

It is poor fun standing to your horses for the best part of the night, and the transport men rather humorously gave voice to this by singing, in excellent harmony and with great fervour, the " Nunc Dimittis " !

We duly moved to, and camped at, Janis, only to be ordered to another camp a mile away on the following day.

The 26th was a pouring wet day, and "A" Squadron were sent to co-operate with the S.R.Y. in a reconnaissance to Doiran station. The reconnaissance was successful. Doiran station was reached and passed, and the patrol proceeded some way to the west until fired on at long range by machine-guns.

One of our horses was hit in the neck, and the bullet, which subsequently was extracted, turned out to be Bulgar—thus confirming the rumour that the Germans had handed over to the Bulgars.

On the 27th a draft of ninety-six men arrived from England and Egypt. These were sent up from the base without proper equipment, or even bivouac sheets. Many of them were Class C men, and had been left in Egypt as being unfit to ride. It was pouring wet, and the ground sodden, and as we were already short of bivouac sheets, little could be done to relieve their discomfort. It was a gross shame ever to have sent them up in this condition.

A GERMAN'S WISH

During the next two days a number of Uhlan and infantry patrols were reported, and the S.R.Y. engaged one, killing two and capturing one. This prisoner was a German, and expressed himself as most anxious to be sent to England, as he had a pal there, a prisoner already. Failing that, he said, he wished to be enlisted as a Royal Engineer!

A Bulgar deserter who was subsequently taken stated that in private life he was an ice-cream vendor in New York, and that he had already deserted successfully in no less than three Balkan wars!

On May 1st great activity was noticed on the part of the enemy, and we could clearly see them constructing new roads and trenches. They signalised the day by firing a few shells at Kilindir with a newly-mounted gun.

On May 4th the Regiment was moved to Erikli, on the east side of the plain, and the opportunity was seized to have a little regimental drill by the way. This was the first opportunity which the Regiment had had of drilling together as a whole since June of the previous year.

Each regiment was now entrusted to the patrol of the whole ridge for ten days at a time in rotation.

On the following day Lieutenant Jackson with his

MAJOR J. G. JOHNSTON, D.S.O.

Commanded " A " Squadron in Salonica

troop pushed a patrol right through Sirlovo and on to the east end of the lake. I believe this was the first occasion on which a British patrol had been into the town, and as Lieutenant Jackson entered it at one end the whole population fled out at the other !

About this time the enemy 'planes became very active, and on the 7th they dropped bombs near " D " Squadron as it was moving up to take its turn at patrolling the ridge, and also dropped two others near our most westerly outpost.

BULGARS AND THE ENGLISH HORSES

The " take over " from the Germans had now apparently been completed, and on the following day Major Winterbottom, commanding " A " Squadron, saw a troop of Bulgars dismounted in the wood below Patros. Taking the Squadron down, he had a regular drive à la covert shoot, but the birds must have broken to a flank, as nothing was seen.

On the way back the squadron were shelled at long range until reaching the crest of the ridge. The shooting was excellent, and it was only by utilising the deep nullahs to the best advantage that the squadron escaped without serious casualties. Pieces of the shells were picked up and proved to belong to 9·2 and 6·7 guns.

On reaching the ridge, a patrol of Bulgar cavalry were seen to leave Sirlovo. These were mounted on small, shaggy ponies, and were armed with rifles only.

On May 10th the Regiment was ordered to provide a flank guard (in the Doiran direction) to the French, who were going to occupy Popovo, some way down the valley to the east. It looked as if the squadron detailed— " D " on this occasion—might have a rough time of it from shell-fire, as they were to spend the whole day in the Patros wood.

Nothing, however, happened, though Patros was shelled immediately after one of our patrols had passed through it. The shooting was again excellent, and the

K

remains of the village, including the policemen's house, were further disintegrated.

The Greek Corporal, who had had a narrow escape, fled up to our outpost line, and incidentally informed me that the Bulgar cavalry had said to him: " The English horses are big and fat, whilst ours are small and thin. It is therefore useless for us to attempt to catch them, so, in future, we will shoot them with the big gun." A really masterly solution of the difficulty on the part of the Bulgar O.C. cavalry!

THUNDERSTORM SPOILS A SCORE

During the remainder of the ten days on the ridge everything possible was done to score a success against enemy patrols, and though for three nights squadrons took it in turns to stay out the whole night, in the hope that the Bulgars were carrying out their patrols under cover of darkness, nothing resulted.

At this time of the year Macedonia is subject to violent thunderstorms and sudden torrential rains, and it was owing to one of the latter that a good opportunity of scoring was lost.

A large patrol of Uhlans had been seen to enter Sirlovo, and they, in fact, came within a few hundred yards of one of our detached posts. In the meantime, the officer in charge, quite rightly, had sent word for his squadron to come up, in the hope of capturing the lot, to attain which his own numbers were totally inadequate. Another five minutes would have done it, when down came a blinding storm, which lasted for half-an-hour, at the end of which time no trace of the enemy could be found.

On the same day Lieutenant Keith was the means of rescuing a party of our gunner officers, who, having foolishly gone on a reconnaissance without telling any of our people (who knew the conditions existing), found themselves cornered by the Bulgars, fortunately in a piece of dead ground, which they were unable to leave.

Observing this, Lieutenant Keith took his troop down from the ridge, and by drawing the enemy's fire, allowed the gunners to escape at a gallop, one by one, and heavily fired at. None of them were hit, which was more than they deserved. This was only due to execrable shooting on the part of the Bulgars. When last seen, the gunners were still galloping past Kilindir!

On May 15th " B " Squadron was sent to take over, from the South Notts, a camp at Orlar, which was a three-days' march to the east, and on the edge of the Struma Valley. This camp was used for instructional purposes in practising cavalry in crossing rivers. There were practically no roads and only the roughest of tracks, and their march was very arduous and difficult for the squadron transport.

On the same day the Regiment was withdrawn, after a very unlucky ten days on the ridge, to a camp two miles north of Kukus, and immediately started on a period of training. Though these periods of training are, of course, a necessity, for troops which are always on patrol quickly get rusty as regards drill, etc., they are nevertheless anything but popular.

On the night of the 18th-19th a number of German 'planes came over, and twenty bombs were dropped, but none fell in our immediate vicinity.

The following day was remarkable for a violent thunderstorm accompanied by hailstones the size of cherries, followed by torrential rain. This only lasted an hour, but by the end of that time the small burn which ran below the camp had become a raging torrent many feet in depth. A limber and four mules belonging to another unit was washed away and the mules drowned. After this I ceased to wonder at the deep fissures ploughed through many feet of soil which one continually came across in the plains.

Monday, May 22nd, to my sorrow, proved to be my last day in command of the Regiment. In the evening we had a football match: Headquarters *versus* " A " Squadron. In the early part of this I was unfortunate enough to fracture a bone in my ankle, and was subsequently invalided home and never rejoined, having been given a special appointment in France. I shall therefore be unable, in the subsequent narrative, to chronicle events from the point of view of an eye-witness, and much detail which I should have liked to have given for the information of those who may read this book years hence will unavoidably be missing.

A FIERCE BATTLE

In a running and chatty diary (NOT the official War Diary) of the Regiment, I have found an account of this football match written after the manner of the *Balkan News*, the official news sheet of the Salonica force. I should like to reproduce it.

NEWS OF THE DAY, 23/5/16

BALKAN FRONT.—The principal item of news is that yesterday evening a fierce battle was fought near Table Hill Camp, Macedonia, between " A " Squadron and a miscellaneous force of Headquarters Troops, Derbyshire Yeomanry. "A's " attacked with spirit and soon gained a trench. H.Q.'s attempted to recover lost ground but were beaten back time and time again. At length they succeeded in driving out the enemy, but in doing so sustained the only casualty of the battle—Colonel Strutt being wounded and carried off the field on a stretcher. Many neutrals watched the conflict and gave expression to critical remarks. They have confidence that by departing from their neutrality they could bring the war to a speedy conclusion. The truth is they have lost their fear of the " Great Powers." The shooting of both sides was poor, and the hand-to-hand and foot-to-foot fighting was not that of highly-trained troops. War Correspondents assert that there was more energy and courage than science and combination.

We understand that neither side can claim any advantage, though both advertise moral victory. H.Q.'s captured various bruises, scratches, etc., and probably the " spoil " claimed by " A's " is quite as important. All the forces have retired to their " dug-outs " to discuss the military situation. On good authority we can state that Iron Crosses, Wooden Spoons, and even higher decorations were conferred upon the following :—

MAJOR SHUTTLEWORTH.—For distinction in defence and marked ability in long-range shooting.

MAJOR WINTERBOTTOM.—For leading a movement on the left flank which passed unnoticed.

LIEUTENANT SWANWICK.—For plentiful expenditure of perspiration.

LIEUTENANT CHETWYND.—For exposing himself to, and stopping, stray shots.

LIEUTENANT FEILDEN.—For valiant charges in the rear of various enemy units.

CORPORAL SMITH.—For continuing to fight though badly wounded in the hand ; for stopping at his post (*viz.*, centre of fire line of reserves) when greatly tempted to move to other parts of the field.

The following may expect early promotion :—

LIEUTENANTS CALDER and ARCHER.—To be foot-drill instructors (Non-Combatant Corps).

SERGEANT-MAJOR PAYNE.—To command company of foot-sloggers.

*SERGEANT REDGATE.—To be Chairman of Local Tribunal.
(*Reuter's Special.*)

(LATER).—There is no truth whatsoever in the report circulated in enemy centres that the non-combatant officer† who was a passenger with Headquarters has been given seven days pack drill for foul language.—*Official.*

MAJOR SHUTTLEWORTH TAKES COMMAND

In the subsequent days camp was moved a short distance for sanitary reasons, as the men were commencing to get dysentery.

Major Shuttleworth now took over temporary command of the Regiment. At the same time several other changes in the personnel of the officers took place. Captain R. M. Wilson, R.A.M.C., and Lieutenant Gillett, machine-gun officer, were both invalided and subsequently sent home, the latter rejoining in the following year. Captain J. M. Taylor, R.A.M.C., and Second-Lieutenant Lowe replaced these two officers in their respective duties. Lieutenant Johnson rejoined from England, and was despatched to Orlar as Second-in-Command of " B " Squadron, whilst Lieutenant Chetwynd, who had been with the Regiment all through, received an appointment in the Egyptian army and left for the base.

---

* Referee.
† The Padre (the Rev. F. H. Ballard).

On the 25th Lieutenant-General Milne, the G.O.C. of the Salonica force, inspected the Regiment in its lines, and was very pleased with everything he saw.

On June 4th the Regiment once more moved to Irikli camp to take over the outpost line for another spell, and " B " Squadron rejoined. With the exception of an occasional shell or two at our outposts there was little incident. The Regiment continued on the ridge until June 20th, when they were relieved by the French Colonial Division.

During this time several football matches were played against other units, in all of which the Regiment was successful. A notable triumph was that over the 12th Cheshires, this being their first defeat since arriving in Macedonia. It is no mean thing for a cavalry regiment, having very little opportunity for footwork, to defeat an infantry battalion of twice its own strength.

Our machine guns were at last changed for the light Vickers gun, and it speaks well for our old guns that they had been in the service of the Regiment for thirteen years and were still in serviceable condition.

CHAPTER XI

SALONICA—*continued*

STRUMA VALLEY

SIMULTANEOUS to handing over the Gola Ridge to the French, the Regiment received orders to march to Kopriva, in the Struma Valley. This was a march of considerable difficulty, especially for the transport, which had to move separately, and by a longer route owing to the absence of roads. For the march the Regiment itself was attended by transport provided by the Indore Company, Indian Mule Transport. The march commenced on June 21st and was completed on the 24th, when the Regiment went into camp one mile north of Kopriva.

Great difficulty was experienced in the crossing of the Spant river, and the Indian transport had a hard time of it. The river was high and the narrow wheels of their light native carts sank deep into the soft sand. The Kruza Balkans, rising to a height of some 2,500 feet, had also to be crossed, and I fancy that by the time camp was reached both men and horses were devoutly thankful. Kopriva lies at the foot of the mountains guarding the south of the Struma Valley, at the point where they most nearly approach the Struma river itself. The town, which is practically midway between the mouth of the river and the Butkova Golu (lake) which I have mentioned as forming the upper end of the valley, and from the upper end of which the river takes a sharp turn to the east and thence flows through the Rupel pass, past Demirhissar, from its source in Bulgaria, is thus only two miles from the river bank, and the same distance south-east of a bridge crossing the river. This bridge was of great importance, being immediately south of the exit from the Rupel pass, thirteen miles north across the plain, and therefore on the direct route of the Bulgars should they advance into Macedonia.

Needless to say, the whole district is extremely unhealthy, and was described in German text books (and rightly as it transpired) as "impossible for European troops to exist in during the summer." It would have been well had our authorities ascertained this fact for themselves, and thereby saved thousands of lives which were lost through the ravages of malaria.

On the 25th Lieut.-Colonel Neilson took over the command of the Regiment, and on the following day Major Carleton returned from leave and resumed his place as Second-in-Command.

On the 27th patrolling was commenced as follows:—

To Alipsa, midway across the plain, to the north-west.

To Demirhissar, on the far side of the plain, to the north.

Nearly to Ceres, to the south-east ; and long distance patrols, lasting three days, were pushed into the hills north-east of the same place.

Up to July 10th these patrols were kept up, though they were handicapped in their movements by being forbidden to penetrate the Greek outpost lines. No action took place, though Bulgar patrols were frequently seen about the mouth of the pass above Demirhissar. At this time, too, German aeroplanes commenced to make frequent and searching visits over our lines, but without bombing our camp.

BOMBED BY A FOKKER

On July 10th the Regiment was marched to Butkova, being bombed by a Fokker on the way, in order to relieve the South Notts, who had been reduced to half their strength by fever. Butkova lies three miles from the eastern end of the shore of the lake of that name, and four miles from its northern end. Patrols were resumed, but without incident, until the 17th, when a patrol, under Lieutenant Willan, was fired on at close range (thirty to fifty yards) from the village of Butkova Dzuma, four miles north of Butkova. The Bulgars must have been very nervous or their shooting execrable, for only one man was hit and that slightly The only possible thing under the circumstances was to gallop for cover as quickly as possible, and, in doing so, considerable confusion was caused by the horses coming down in a blind ditch. The French artillery, with their usual courtesy, immediately shelled the village as soon as we were clear of it, though our artillery, who were over a mile nearer, did not fire a shot. It appears that at that time our artillery had orders not even to fire a registering round—presumably for fear of hitting a Bulgar and irritating him or of hurting the feelings of the Greeks. Whatever the cause, it appeared to those taking part that the war was to be a somewhat one-sided affair.

On July 19th a few cases of fever are mentioned for the first time, not only from within the two squadrons at Butkova, but also in " A " Squadron, which had been left at Kopriva.

On the following day there is another entry, " Fever increasing at Kopriva," and on the 23rd, "Great increase of fever." On 24th, " thirty-six cases to hospital " ; 25th, " thirty-six cases to hospital " ; 27th, " twenty-three to hospital " ; whilst on the next four days the average was eighteen per diem. So that within the first week of its appearance 167 men were sent to hospital out of a strength of about 400. The Regiment had taken every precaution, had taken quinine before entering the fever zone, had camped on the highest available ground, had burnt all grass and bushes round the camp, and had repeatedly applied, without result, for mosquito netting.

By the 31st Brigade Headquarters were depleted of both the Brigadier and Brigade-Major, and had forty-five men down out of between sixty and seventy.

The Derbyshire and South Notts Regiments were
so reduced in strength that it was decided to amalgamate
into one regiment, and by this means three weak squadrons of eighty men each were formed out of the two
regiments, and the superfluous horses were sent back
to a horse camp under Captain Birchenough.

By August 1st the eighty men per squadron were
reduced to seventy.   Infantry battalions of normally
800 were, in some cases, reduced to a total strength of
one hundred men.

A Brigade depot was then formed at Lahana.

On the 19th " A " Squadron joined the Sherwood
Rangers in order to repel a Bulgar descent into the
plain from Demirhissar.   Some fighting, of which I
can obtain no details, took place, and some casualties
were sustained.

HEAVY FIGHTING

By the 20th the Bulgars were well down into the
plain, and a series of strong reconnaissances were made
to ascertain their strength and dispositions.

These entailed some heavy fighting, lasting most of
the day, during which a number of casualties occurred.
" A " Squadron came in for the thick of it, and a very
gallant troop action took place which resulted in almost
the entire loss of that troop.   During this action Captain
Johnson, who really had no business to have participated,
behaved with great gallantry, thereby winning the
D.S.O.   I will describe this troop action and the events
leading up to it in the words of Lieutenant W. M. B.
Feilden, who commanded the troop, and who was one
of the few survivors, himself being wounded.

On August 18th, about 2 p.m., I received orders to go to
Kopriva and form the patrol in the direction of Barakli
Dzama, and find out how far the Bulgars had advanced in
the previous night.   I arrived at Kopriva 5 p.m., and found
about two or three thousand French troops there who had
" retired "—(I understand that this " retirement " was
hurried to say the least of it.—Ed.)—from Ceres.   I got
what information I could from them, and then sent Lieut.
Noel (Intelligence Officer) with eight men to Elisan to get in

touch with the French there, and took the remainder of the troop to Ormanli. The village was not occupied, but we were fired on by Bulgars to the north of the village. It was nearly dark by this time, so I decided to return to Kopriva via the south end of Barakli Dzama and Dolop Ciftli; both these places were strongly held.

I got back to Kopriva about 9 p.m. Two horses died on arrival there from colic set up by bits of steel put into the oats. (Steel oats were a favourite trick of the Boche, though they were usually detected as they sank to the bottom of the sack. They were, of course, introduced in America or Canada.—Ed.)

I had orders to remain at Kopriva that night, but at 4 a.m. received further orders to join " A " Squadron at Orljak. On arrival there, the horses were too beat to go out with the Squadron, and I remained in camp that day.

At 3 a.m. on the morning of the 20th, " A " Squadron left Orljak for Kopriva, with orders to reconnoitre Elisan, Kumli, Prosenik, etc., and act on the left of the French, who, I believe, had orders to retake all the villages they had retired from on the 18th.

The Squadron reached Elisan at 6 a.m. From there I had orders from G. W. (Major Guy Winterbottom—Ed.) to reconnoitre Kumli. This was held by about twenty Bulgars, who retired after firing a few shots.

Capt. G. Johnson was then sent up to Kumli to reinforce me, and after I had ridden through the village and reported all clear to him, G. W. arrived with the rest of the Squadron about 10 a.m. He proceeded to water and feed the horses, and sent me into the village to buy what provisions I could. Whilst I was there, a large force, apparently, of Bulgars, had crept up through the maize on the east side of Kumli and rushed the outpost there. When I got out of the village there was not a soul in sight, nor a sign of " A " Squadron, as they had retired and taken up a position in a sunk road a quarter-of-a-mile south-west of Kumli. (As a matter of fact, not only were the Bulgars in the village with Lieut. Feilden, but they went so far as to pinch his field glasses and mackintosh which he had left lying on a wall whilst he was in a house.—Ed.)

AN EXCITING ESCAPE

G. W. rode back for me as the Bulgars were then coming through the village, and took me up on the back of his horse, but no sooner had he done so than the horse reared up and fell backwards with us both. The Bulgars were then very close indeed, but Trumpeter Joynt rode out and took me up on the back of his horse, and G. W. retired all right on his own. After a good deal of fighting, the Squadron retired to take up a better position north of Elisan.

From there Lieut. Willan, with four men, was sent out to try and ascertain the strength of the enemy in Kumli, and was heavily fired on with rifles and machine guns. He estimated their strength to be about 2,000, but, from a prisoner who was taken later, it appeared that their strength was 6,000 infantry alone, not to mention cavalry and guns.

The total strength of " A " Squadron when we left Orljak in the morning was about eighty-five all told.

We were ordered to hold Elisan at all costs, and were reinforced by two companies of infantry. These companies had been marching for several days, and what with sickness and other causes, had been reduced to something like thirty men per company.

The two companies were under the command of an infantry Major, who took over the command of Elisan from G. W.

By about 7 p.m. a considerable number of Bulgars were working their way round our left flank, and looked as if they might cut off Elisan from Brigade Headquarters at Kopriva bridge.

I was ordered to take my troop to a sunk road about 300 yards to the north-west of Elisan, and to hold on to that flank.

After being there for a short time, G. Johnson brought me orders to mount my troop and go and charge a party of Bulgars, about thirty to fifty in number, who were in the open and working round our left flank about one mile north-west of Elisan. (These orders were issued by the infantry Major, and it is very doubtful, under the circumstances, whether they should ever have been given.—Ed.)

I mounted the troop, and advanced in extended order. So soon as we left the sunk road a terrific fire was opened on us. I looked back soon after we had started and saw that G. Johnson, instead of going back to the Squadron at Elisan, had turned round and was coming on too. After going for a quarter mile we came to a deep ditch about ten yards wide, with a high bank on the landing side. This was grown up with bullrushes, and when we jumped into the middle of it the horses sank up to their bellies in the mud. However, I believe that everyone got over all right. I got hit in the leg shortly after this, and I fancy that most of the troop had been put out of action by this time. Fifty yards from the enemy I gave the order—CHARGE.

There were five men left then, and, as far as I can remember, they were Sergeant Briggs, H. Crowder, A. Holt, Corporal Weston, and the name of the fifth man I do not remember. They were magnificent, and let out a roar like lions, but every one of them was rolled over. I was shot again at point blank range, and, as my horse was badly hit in five places and the off-side reins shot through, I thought it time to leave.

Sergeant Briggs had, I believe, three horses shot under him in this show. As often as his own horse was hit, he caught another loose horse, and had no sooner mounted that than he was hit through the leg and his horse killed; he managed to catch another horse but that was killed when he had only ridden back a short way. G. Johnson and Corporal Abbott then got hold of Sergeant Briggs, and between them they managed to get several of the wounded men back, being heavily fired on the whole while. It appears that besides the party of Bulgars in the open whom I was ordered to charge, there was also a force of several hundred in the maize close by, and it was this force which did most of the damage.

For some unknown reason they stayed where they were that night, but had they come on things might have been very serious indeed.

The troop was about twenty strong when we started. Lance-Corporal Wright, Corporal Weston, Troopers Austin, H. H. Hall, P. W. Hall, A. Holt, and Mansfield were either killed or missing. Sergeant Briggs, Lance-Corporal Saddington, Trooper Ironmonger and S.S. Milne were wounded, Trooper Crowder taken prisoner, and S.S. Bott shell shock. The remainder of the troop all had their horses shot but managed to get back themselves.

The above story speaks for itself, and no elaboration on my part could add to the gallantry or glory of the attempt. Any cavalry regiment in the world might well be proud to have this story recorded in its pages.

I may add, however, that Lieutenant Feilden got back all right by galloping his horse in a left-hand circle on the near rein, falling off it from exhaustion just as he passed a stretcher party. One of his first recollections was of the amusement caused him by the sight of Gerald Johnson beating along his wounded horses with the flat of his sword when taking part in the charge.

CONSTANTLY IN TOUCH

Between August 20th and the first week in September much patrolling was carried out, during which time the remains of " A " Squadron were constantly in touch with the enemy. A depot for the Regiment was formed at Gevezne, and " B " Squadron, with the addition of two squadrons of Lothian and Border Horse, namely

" D " and " C, " joined up with " A " Squadron, thus forming a new composite regiment. It must be remembered that fever was still at its height, thus making it utterly impossible to anything like complete any one regiment. Headquarters were established at Kopachi, which is east of the main Ceres road, and in the Struma Valley. An outpost line was now formed along the river front. These outpost positions were fortified and comparatively strong, and were designed to protect the bridges over the Struma, which were, of course, vital to us, and also any parts of the river where it might be possible for the Bulgars to cross either by fording or by bridging. These apparently had the desired effect, for nothing worthy of record occurred until September 10th.

During August things in general appeared to have taken rather a turn in our favour. To begin with, on June 21st the Allies had presented a note to Greece, and this had been accepted. The chief item which affected the Salonica force was the demand to commence the demobilisation of their army.

The note was agreed to, and the demobilisation commenced (probably without much reluctance on the part of the army itself). On August 27th Roumania came into the war on our side, and this fact alone inspired great hopes. This was immediately followed, on the 30th, by a popular rising in favour of Venizelos, which in a very short time led to the enrolment of a Greek pro-allied army. This army received recruits in numbers. Its training was immediately put in hand under the supervision of the British and French, with the result that by the middle of 1917 it was ready in all respects to play an important part in the theatre of operations. Some time previous to this the remnants of the Serbian army had been collected, reorganised, and re-trained, with the result that by the autumn of this year they were in a position to be given a part of the line to maintain, and, as the general history of the war will prove, were destined to take a decisive part in the eventual success of the allied arms.

On September 10th things once more began to wake up, and on that day a demonstration was made across the river. The Yeomanry force consisted of " A " Squadron Derbys with one squadron each of South Notts and Sherwood Rangers. This force crossed by a cable ferry, which had been erected, " A " Squadron advancing towards Godeli and returning without casualties, whilst the other two squadrons of the composite regiment made a demonstration towards Orljak bridge. No action of any importance took place, and the Bulgars contented themselves with heavily shelling the whole of our sector.

A SUCCESSFUL DEMONSTRATION

A few patrol encounters took place during the next few days, and on the 16th another demonstration was made under the command of Lieut.-Colonel Neilson. The cavalry this time consisted of two squadrons of the Derbys and two squadrons of the Lothian and Border Horse, and co-operated with the 29th Infantry Brigade.

The demonstration was completely successful, and the enemy suffered a number of casualties.

The Yeomanry crossed the river, and under cover of our artillery fire attacked both Kato Godeli and Anna Godeli, and after meeting with only slight opposition, which was easily crushed, captured both villages. These were then set on fire and held by us until dark, when the force re-crossed the river successfully.

In the meantime the 29th Brigade carried out an attack on Zammamah, which resulted in further loss for the enemy and the destruction of several of their posts. It further transpired that this demonstration caused a force of Bulgars to retire from Omertacli. This force was observed by our gunners and was heavily shelled, with good results.

On the 17th the Regiment moved from Kopaci to Badimal, two miles to the east. All the places which I have mentioned recently will be found on the map immediately south of the northern end of the Tabinos sea and on the south bank of the Struma river. The river recently mentioned as having been crossed on several occasions is not the main Struma river, but one of its several estuaries.

The Bulgars, after driving out the French from Ceres, had advanced across the plain, crossed the Struma in places, and were now endeavouring to establish themselves in the mountains to the south. Up to this date they had not made any serious attempt to attack them, and had merely contented themselves with establishing lines of posts in the villages south of the river, and with holding these as an advanced outpost line pending the attack which was believed to be preparing against our positions in the hills.

On the 23rd another raid was organised, the force on this occasion consisting of the Sherwood Rangers, one squadron of Lothians, and one squadron Derbys, together with an infantry force. The objective was much the same as that on the 16th, and entailed the capture of Kato and Anna Godeli and Zammamah.

This time things went wrong from the start, and the Sherwoods, who were detailed for the capture of the two former villages, were delayed from advancing against Kato owing to faulty direction of our covering artillery fire. They succeeded in capturing Anna Godeli after meeting with some opposition, but were soon driven out again. A lot of sniping commenced on the left flank, and the Derbys, under Captain Rawlinson, were detailed to deal with this. It was impossible to subdue the sniping, for it must be borne in mind that not only is this country very rough and broken wherever the ground rises at all steeply, but that it is thickly cultivated, chiefly with crops of maize rising to seven feet in height, wherever it is flat. Accordingly the only possible course was to advance as far as practicable so as to induce the snipers to withdraw out of effective range of the main force, and then to form a line, so as to keep them there, and wait until operations were over.

CAPTAIN LORD G. F. A. VERNON

*Second in Command " B " Squadron.   Invalided from
Gallipoli, and died at Malta, 1915*

On a cold and pouring wet day such as this was,
" B " Squadron had no mean task of endurance set
them, and they performed it well.   It is a very different
thing to be shot at during the excitement of an attack
to being shot at by snipers whom you cannot see, and
against whom you are unable to retaliate.   When this
goes on for several hours, during which your only
possible rôle is to sit still and endure it, all the time
getting colder and wetter, it simply resolves itself into
a test of discipline.   Troops who can stand this sort
of thing can usually stand most things.   Though the
fire was not heavy, it was continuous, and three men
were wounded.

A CURIOUS ENGAGEMENT

A curious engagement took place on the 30th which
well illustrates the difficulties of independent operations
in a country of this nature, and, of course, the necessity
for all troops in the vicinity having an accurate knowledge of anything afoot.   On this occasion Colonel
Neilson crossed the river at the Gudeli Ferry, and meeting
with a few snipers cleared them out without casualties.
Immediately afterwards he came under a hot rifle
fire from the South Notts, which, after curses, ob-
jurgations and a general exchange of compliments
down the telephone, presently ceased.   In the meantime,
Major Carleton, who was commanding the supports on
the river bank, was alarmed and probably disconcerted
on witnessing the stampede of a party of our infantry
who believed that they had been surrounded.   This
effect was brought about not only by the fire of the
South Notts, but by that of enemy snipers whose shots
were mostly falling short, whilst the " ricochets " were
landing over.   Matters, however, were soon cleared up,
and, as the diary remarks, " the usual week-end river
party tranquillity once more reigned," though this
tranquillity was somewhat marred by the unexpected
arrival of some Bulgar shrapnel which, falling to the
right of the Derbys, wounded one of the South Notts

L.

During the day the latter had four men killed and three wounded.

I chiefly mention the foregoing scrap to show how easy it is on occasions for a scare to start. It need only originate from one man, but may easily spread in magnitude until it becomes of first-rate importance.

The British had numerous agents within the Bulgar lines, and about this time one of them, an ex-Greek soldier residing in Ceres, sent in a rather illuminating document in respect to the raid made by the Derbys on the 16th.

This document goes to show that on occasions the Bulgars, like our own Tommies, develop a somewhat fertile brain when describing an action. It reads as follows : " The Bulgars fled home panic stricken from the English, *who bayoneted fifty of them*. The English then walked about setting fire to the villages, striking matches and smoking *cigars* the while." (The italics are mine.)

A NEW PHASE

October came, and with it the campaign took a new phase, for on the 1st and 2nd our infantry attacked across the plain. No opportunity for cavalry fighting occurred, and for two days the Regiment had a rest. Artillery fire was very heavy and continuous. Our infantry pushed their way across the river and established themselves on the northern bank, which they succeeded in holding, in spite of numerous heavy counter-attacks by the enemy. During these attacks the Bulgars suffered heavy casualties from our gunners, posted as they were amongst the hills which overlooked the plain. Fighting centred itself for a long time around Jenikoi, which changed hands time after time. On the evening of the 3rd the Regiment received orders to join the Reserve of the 27th Division at once. By 8.30 p.m. they were off, and had reached their destination by 9.45 p.m. Here they were halted, awaiting developments, on the bare hillside. The night was spent here in great discomfort, as, in addition to a wind, there was a sharp frost, the first of the approaching winter.

At this date the strength of the Regiment, all told, was: " A " Squadron, sixty-five; " B " Squadron, seventy-one. " C " Squadron was still at Gevezne refitting. The 4th and 5th found them standing by in Corps Reserve, *i.e.*, the 16th Corps, to which Corps the Regiment had been attached a month previously, and with which it served till the conclusion of war. During these days attacks and counter-attacks on Jenïkoi and Karadzakoi continued without intermission, until finally both were left in our hands.

On the 6th the Regiment were once more employed on patrolling, and patrols were pushed out to the front of Kalendia and Homondos, where the enemy were found in force, and were subsequently attacked by our armoured cars. The Regiment returned via Jenïkoi, which they found a mass of debris and full of dead.

On the 8th another reconnaissance was made, and this time the Regiment, crossing the river at Komarian and marching through Osman Kamilla and Kospeki, reached the embankment of the Ceres railway. Here they came under shell fire, and Corporal Auckland, whose horse was shot on the embankment, was taken prisoner. After this reconnaissance the Regiment returned to camp at Kopachi, only to be moved to Osman Kamilla the following day.

On the 11th of October the Regiment moved to Ada, and no sooner had they got into camp than they were turned out at 1 a.m., on the report that the enemy were evacuating Ceres. They moved off to investigate, but on arriving within 600 yards of the railway embankment, were fired on with a heavy but misdirected fire, and returned to camp.

They were again sent out at 9.30 the same morning, and, after turning a party of twelve Bulgar cavalry, who, in the preceding days, had succeeded in holding up each of the other regiments in turn, from Tumbitza, pushed on across the railway, which had now been evacuated, in pursuit of the retreating enemy. Failing to get in touch with them, and as by now the horses were pretty far through, they returned to camp to find it all packed up and in readiness to move. A report had come that the Bulgars were preparing to attack from Ceres, but when the threatened attack was boiled down to the retirement of twenty Bulgars from Nihor, who incidentally only just escaped capture by the South Notts, no one was best pleased. It is poor fun returning home after a long day and after a sleepless night to find that your home has, for the moment, ceased to be.

ADVENT OF GREEKS

On the following day the first mention is made of Greeks fighting on our side. Perhaps I am wrong when I say "fighting," for on this occasion they, and a band of our comitadjis, spoiled what was intended for a day of rest by raising an unnecessary alarm.

The usual patrols were again resumed, but now further north than formerly. The Bulgars had apparently decided to give up the actual plain, but still held the hills to the north. No incident occurred for a week.

On the 17th, to everybody's joy, " C " Squadron (formerly " D ") rejoined at full strength, and with them they brought a batch of reinforcements for the other two squadrons. This brought the Regiment practically up to establishment once more ; a most welcome change for all.

The three squadrons were now officered as follows :

" A."—Major Winterbottom, Captain Johnson, Lieutenants Jackson and Low, Second-Lieutenant Wilson.

" B."—Major Shuttleworth, Captain Rawlinson, Lieutenants Branfill, Drury, Gilpin, and Blatch.

" C."—Major Clark, Captain Birchenough, Lieutenant Buckston.

On the 19th " A " Squadron laid a successful ambush for a Bulgar patrol at Ciftli Tefik, which resulted in one prisoner and three or four more killed or wounded.

No further action of any sort took place before the end of the month, and the Regiment was withdrawn to Kopachi, where it was given a good and well earned rest.

Hitherto I have given patrol actions in some detail, as I wished not only to bring out their varied nature, but the constant work, without rest, for both man and horse. Though these patrols may not have led to serious engagements or heavy casualties, they, nevertheless, meant that practically every day, providing that a patrol did its work conscientiously, some troop or other would come under fire—it might be at close range from a patch of maize, or it might be from snipers at long range, but that matters not at all, for the arrival of a bullet if it meets its billet has the same result. It is impossible for anyone to go out on patrol, even though everything appeared to be perfectly quiet and normal, and yet to call his life his own until he reaches camp again at nightfall. In addition to this, it must be remembered that camp was being continually changed, which entails no little trouble and exertion, and that even when things were quiet and the men were nominally having an " easy," yet a considerable proportion of them had always to be " standing to," waiting to go out should any emergency arise. Having realised this, you will understand that a cavalry regiment doing patrol duties has a really hard time. When two forces are stationary, to all intents and purposes, the rôle of the cavalry is not only to protect the infantry by day, by a system of either outposts or patrols, usually both, but at night, when the infantry takes over, though the outposts and patrols have nominally ceased for the moment, it has to be ready to move at a moment's notice should an emergency arise. In fact—unless actually and officially withdrawn for a rest—neither their lives nor their time is their own for a moment.

HARD WORK WELL DONE

Remember at the same time that the work during the summer of 1916 was carried out under intense heat, that the Regiment was for most of the time reduced to a shadow owing to sickness, that it was working in a country which the Germans had declared was impossible for European troops to exist in, and that more than half of those with the Regiment at any one time had suffered from malaria and were likely to be attacked by it again at any moment, and you will realise that the work done by the Notts and Derby Mounted Brigade was of no mean order. That it was carried out successfully and to the satisfaction of those in the highest command is entirely due to the magnificent material of which the British Yeomanry were composed.

So far as possible, squadrons took turn and turn about for patrol duties, excepting, of course, such days when the whole Regiment was out on some major operation.

When one squadron was absent for any length of time, extra work was naturally thrown on the others, and this was the case all the time during which " C " Squadron was refitting.

The average day's patrol is a long one, for it is usually advisable to be well on to one's ground by daybreak. This in the summer means reveille somewhere about three o'clock in the morning ; the squadron marching about 4.30, according to the hours of daylight. Having pushed up to some suitable place, where water can be had for the horses, and within the edge of the debatable ground, the squadron halts and pushes out patrols, remaining where it is as their support in case of trouble.

The patrols usually remain out for most of the day, either pushing well out if no opposition is met with, or lying up watching for an opportunity of surprising a hostile patrol, or in watching the movements of the enemy.

On most days they are fired on—it may be from a few snipers which have to be hunted out before further progress can be made, or it may be by a hostile patrol holding some village and thus debarring the rest of the plain to our patrol. Here, again, the village has to be made good, and frequently on a threat of turning the flanks of the village, the enemy patrol will bolt.

There is always the possibility of its being held by a considerable force, and then the patrol may find itself " up against it " in several ways.

The squadron, or what is left of it, may or may not be called upon to act. Even if they are not, their day will probably be enlivened by the arrival of a few shells in their vicinity some time during the day.

In a country such as the Struma Valley nothing can be left to chance, or disaster will be courted. Every patch of maize may hold some of the enemy, and must be approached as if it was known to do so. Similarly, because a village was found to contain no enemy yesterday, it must not for a moment be taken as granted that it does not do so to-day. Constant vigilance is an absolute essential if undue casualties are to be avoided. The men naturally became extremely expert at this sort of work, but, expert or not, the life was a most trying one.

Camp will probably not be reached till dusk ; horses have to be watered, fed and groomed before the men are free to turn in after probably an eighteen hours' working day, with, very likely, the prospect of an early move of the whole camp, with all the packing up which that entails, in the morning.

If the night is otherwise peaceful, you will still have the mosquitoes to contend with, or, towards the middle of October, a sharp frost which makes your blanket seem remarkably thin.

The short rest ended on October 30th, and on that day the Regiment left Kopachi, and, crossing the Kumarian bridge, slept the night at Osman Kamilla. On the following day the whole Brigade was moved eastward to demonstrate on the line Nihor, Tumbitza, Virhanli, whilst the 28th Division were carrying out an attack on Barakli Dzuma. The Brigade was heavily

shelled at its rendezvous, and no time was wasted in
" getting a move on."

The Regiment moved to Kakaraska, where it joined
up with a company of Greeks and a squadron of
Chasseurs d'Afrique, also a battery of 75's. Patrols and
" feelers " were thrust out all day against the wood
known as " Pheasant Wood," and in the evening Major
Winterbottom with two troops tried to investigate
Tumbitza, but was compelled to retire. In the evening
all returned to Kopachi, with the exception of " C "
Squadron, which was left behind to sleep at Ago Mah.
During the day several horses were hit, and Trooper
Hastie was shot through the thigh.

During the following week, that is, the first week of
November, nothing occurred except that " C " Squadron
was successful in capturing a Bulgar patrol of a sergeant
and four men.

On the 17th the Regiment moved to Kakaraska, and
lay there in support of the infantry, who made an attack
on Tumbitza on the 18th. This attack failed.

CHAPTER XII

SALONICA—*continued*

IN WINTER QUARTERS

SHORTLY after this, the Regiment were glad to take a leaf out of Julius Cæsar's book and to "withdraw into winter quarters." This sounds better than it really was, for one squadron was left on the line Salma to Kakaraska or at Jenikoi, in order to watch Prosenik, Topolva and Kumli.

"Going into winter quarters" sounds very nice and restful after a long, trying and arduous summer on the plains, but apparently it was on this occasion only one of the numerous "leg pulls" which G.H.Q. occasionally indulged in, for in less than a week's time we find the Regiment back in its old haunts, and lying in support at Janimah and Kospeki, with a squadron at each place, during an infantry attack on Tumbitza. On the following morning, December 7th, we find them once again in action. At 6 a.m. the Regiment moved off at the trot from Kato Godeli to a sunken road which lies a little north of Pheasant Wood. Their orders were to gallop on reaching this point, to cross the Tumbitza ford, and thence round so as to take Vinhanli in the rear. All went well, and though the Regiment came under very heavy shell fire for ten minutes, only two men and six horses were hit. At night the Regiment returned to Kospeki.

After a further short spell of so-called rest the Regiment was marched, on the 12th, westwards to its old haunts around Orljak. Arriving there, they once again took up an outpost line extending from Kumli through Prosenik to Homendos, and here they remained all winter, each squadron taking on the duties of the outpost line in rotation.

On the 29th it looked as if we were to find ourselves involved in yet another war; for reservists of the Greek Royalist Regiments, who were now well behind us, and theoretically in the process of demobilisation, commenced to wage war on us. The trouble was soon quashed, however, though not without fighting in which the Regiment participated.

On the morning of that day " C " Squadron, under Major D'Arcy Clark, was suddenly ordered to move, together with the South Notts, to operate against these reservists on the line Stavros to Langavuk. The movement was quickly carried out, and an engagement resulted with loss to the Greeks amounting to seven killed, a number wounded, and forty-six prisoners. The squadron rejoined at Orljak after a fortnight's absence.

The New Year found the Regiment still on the same outpost line, the squadron on duty seeing Bulgars and being under rifle or shell fire from them on most days.

The squadron on duty across the river took spells of four days in duration, and this allowed for an eight days' rest for that which had last returned from duty. During each period of rest a scheme of training was carried out, and much time was devoted to musketry. In addition to this, the Regiment had just been given twelve Hotchkiss guns, and the training of their detachments was at once taken in hand.

The whole of January passed without incident worthy of special mention, with the exception of the assistance given by one troop to the infantry in a successful little foray on Kupri, which resulted in a loss to the Bulgars of two killed, two wounded, and twenty-eight unwounded prisoners.

When I say that no special incidents took place I do not wish readers to infer, wrongfully, that any period was devoid of action, or that the holding of an outpost or patrol line is a sinecure. During January and on into February, though I have made no special mention of them, patrol actions were almost of daily occurrence, and failing such an action the squadron on duty was pretty certain to be shelled.

For instance, on February 2nd forty-eight shells were fired at the troop in Prosenik, whilst on the following day a determined attack was made by about sixty Bulgars on the same place. This attack was pressed well home, and was only beaten back by rifle fire after they had advanced to within 200 yards.

Were I to give accounts of every patrol action, this book would be interminable. My excuse for having already mentioned or described so many is to bring home to the reader the diversity of the operations. One day it may be a flank guard ; another, a demonstration to hold the enemy from giving assistance elsewhere ; on another, a combined operation with the infantry, the Regiment either acting as support or as mounted infantry or as a turning force ; the following day may produce a series of patrol encounters on the outpost line, whilst the next may be a raid on some village, or merely an information-seeking patrol. Each day, in fact, may have, and frequently does have, something fresh in store. No better practical training ground could be found—for odd shells and bullets are the best of instructors and allow for no hesitation, insisting, in fact, on the right movement and its being carried out instanter.

It is no wonder, then, that by the winter of 1916 the Yeomanry Regiments in Macedonia were not only ready, but able to go anywhere and to do practically anything.

During February the Regiment was allowed to go into a much-needed and well-earned rest, which lasted until March 3rd, when it once more found itself on outpost on the old line, namely, Kalendra, Prosenik, Kumli and Barakli. Here it remained for a fortnight, during which time outpost encounters were of everyday occurrence, whilst, to vary the monotony, the Bulgars heavily shelled the whole outpost line on the 17th.

Unfortunately, during this spell several cases of sarcoptic mange appeared amongst the horses, and this, for some time onwards, considerably increased the difficulties, and the work within the Regiment, entailing, as it did, the isolation of not only the actual cases, but of the suspected cases as well and the frequent dressing of all horses in the Regiment.

Hitherto the Regiment had had practically complete absence of all skin complaints within the horse lines, and when it is remembered that for long periods body and dandy brushes were most difficult to come by, and that clippers and fresh blades for the same were even more so, great credit must be given not only to the troop officers, but equally to the N.C.O.'s and men for this immunity.

Without most careful and conscientious grooming outbreaks are bound to occur, and, speaking from personal experience gained later on in France, it requires very little lack of attention for a unit to put itself practically out of action within a remarkably short space of time owing to lack of proper grooming.

At the end of the third week of March the Regiment handed over the outpost line to the 10th Division, and moved to Kopachi, where it occupied the same ground vacated by it on December 12th of the previous year. Here they remained until April 10th, the whole of the intervening time being occupied in troop and squadron training.

IN THE FRONT LINE

On the 10th the Regiment moved to Dzamimah, where they relieved the Sherwood Rangers in the front line of the sector extending from Regikmah on the south-east to a point cutting the track from Aromah to Seres on the north-west.

Each squadron in turn took over the outpost line of this sector for spells of three days, and four posts were provided, or five, counting the Squadron Headquarters, and one troop at Kispeki. At first this sector of the line was held by the 2nd D.C.L.I., and later by the 2nd Gloucesters.

At first little movement on the part of the enemy was observed, but on the 15th patrols pushing out towards Tombitsa and Virhanli were fired on from a bluff overlooking the latter place, and within a few days it became apparent that the enemy had every intention of hanging on there as they were seen to be busily engaged in trenching and wiring, and this activity increased as the days passed.

Major Tremayne now took over the command of the Regiment in place of Lieut.-Colonel Neilson, who was given command of the Brigade. On this line, as elsewhere, the outposts were in action every day, but suffered very few casualties, though Lieutenant Vaughan was wounded on the 17th whilst endeavouring to cut off with his troop a party of Bulgars retiring from Arabadzik.

This line was held until May 14th (for the last three days both by night and day), when the South Notts Hussars took over, and the Regiment retired once more to Kopachi for rest and the usual training. The establishment of the horses was now increased up to 475, thus bringing the Regiment up to cavalry establishment.

On June 1st the Regiment once more moved up to Dzamimah and took over their former patrol line from the South Notts—who, together with the Sherwoods, were marched down country on the 19th, being eventually sent to Palestine.

The Brigade, which had been together now for almost three years, was now definitely broken up, and the Derbyshire Yeomanry, thus left alone, became a part of the 16th Corps.

For reasons both tactical and sanitary the infantry now retired from the whole of the ground on the north side of the Struma, and occupied a line on its right, or south, bank. In accordance with this new line, the Headquarters of the Regiment now moved into camp at Ismailli, where it remained with two squadrons in rotation—the third going into camp at Turica for six-day spells, from which place it patrolled a line, formerly within our lines, running from north to south through Mazirko—Yenikoi—Cuculuk—Elisan and on to Alipsa.

DANGEROUS PATROL LINE

This patrol line proved to be the most difficult and dangerous which had as yet been encountered. The scrub was thick, and, at this season of the year, over extensive areas of cultivated ground, the maize stood at a great height. Eyes, however keen and practised, were practically useless, as it was absolutely easy for the enemy to lie hidden until our patrols were literally within a few yards.

The only possible method of procedure, therefore, was simply to push ahead—if you were not fired on a report could safely be made that that immediate area was clear of enemy—usually the converse was the case. Under these circumstances casualties amongst the patrols became much more frequent ; that this was so only proves that the work was well and conscientiously done, for it is a great temptation and frequently quite easy for a patrol to avoid a particularly nasty looking place and to take the enemy's absence as granted.

NUMEROUS CASUALTIES

Within a few days the following casualties took place. On the 16th Private Haywood and Private Pearson were wounded on patrol, whilst on the following day Private Smith was wounded and Private Connor killed near Yenikoi. Connor, when hit, was brought out of action in a most gallant manner by Corporal Dungworth and Private Walker, but died on the 19th. I am glad to record the sequel to this, for on the 26th the Corps Commander conferred the Military Medal on both these men for conspicuous gallantry.

On the 23rd, Private Labon, whilst patrolling near Toplova, was seen to fall from his horse after being fired on and was reported missing ; exactly the same thing happened to Private Thornby two days later. So it went on day after day—Corporal Hanson was killed near Haznatar, Privates G. Eley and H. Large were wounded at the same place, and S.S. Appleby was seriously wounded and Major Winterbottom slightly wounded near Cuculuk.

During this period no incident worthy of record took place, and, though on more than one occasion we assisted the infantry in raids, on each occasion the enemy promptly cleared out. The nature of the ground suited the Bulgars in their guerilla tactics most admirably, as, from their point of view, lying up in the best of cover for a " sitting shot " at a patrol was an infinitely better, and decidedly safer, game to play than attempting to contest a village which they did not really in the least want with infantry and yeomen infinitely better trained than themselves.

On July 2nd Regimental-Sergeant-Major Nelson, who had done good service with the Regiment not only in Macedonia, but also in the early part of the war as Squadron-Sergeant-Major, left the Regiment for the coast, and so to England, owing to the completion of his term of service. Shortly after his arrival home he obtained a well-deserved commission.

On August 2nd one of our patrols got a bit of its own back. On the points of the patrol approaching a redoubt about 400 yards south of Dolop, they were fired on and immediately retired. This was too great a temptation for the Bulgars, and two of them immediately jumped up on to the edge of the parapet in order to get a better shot at their foe. This opportunity was not missed by the patrol, which had a Hotchkiss gun, and one of the Bulgars was dropped fair and square. On seeing this a mounted patrol of Bulgars forthwith galloped from behind the redoubt and made for a neighbouring wood. The patrol numbered six, but only two succeeded in reaching the cover which they sought.

MAJOR WINTERBOTTOM KILLED

August 9th was a black-letter day for the whole Regiment, not only for those on actual service with it at the time, but for all those other members of it who were either serving at home or had been invalided back. On this day Major Guy Winterbottom met his death. His squadron was out doing its turn of patrol, and he was out visiting a chain of posts which he had established. Riding from one to another, he was fired on at long range (estimated at 800 yards) from somewhere between Elisan and Cuculuk, and was hit mortally, dying soon afterwards.

This very gallant officer and best type of English gentleman had done magnificent work with the Regiment throughout the war. He appeared to be absolutely fearless, though well realising the dangers, was invariably cheerful, and was beloved by both officers and men equally. He was one of that type of officer who could be relied upon to carry out any order not only in the letter but in the spirit. Though absent from the Regiment at this time, I know full well that it can never have been quite the same again after Guy's death. That the men almost invariably called him Guy behind his back was a sure proof of their devotion and an earnest that they would have followed him anywhere. What better could anyone desire or deserve? To those who served with him or under him his name and the remembrance of his friendship will ever recall the happiest of memories.

During the next few days a number of men and one officer were wounded during patrol encounters. A patrol towards Cuculuk came under fire and one man was wounded by the Bulgars, who held the village with a force of from forty to fifty men. On the following day they lay up in the trenches and awaited our patrol, reserving their fire until it got within a few yards. Only one man, Private Mort, was hit, or presumed to be hit, as he was taken prisoner, though his horse was regained and showed several bullet wounds. A few

MAJOR C. A. BRANFILL, M.C.

Commanded " C " Squadron, 1918 until 1919

days later Lieutenant Bowmer was wounded by a bomb thrown from a house in Elisan.

BULGARS' BAD SHOOTING

The wonder is that our casualties were not very much heavier, and this can only be attributed to appallingly bad shooting on the part of the enemy. Had the boot been on the other leg and the Bulgars been compelled to send out information-seeking patrols, their is no doubt that their patrols would have either been practically wiped out or that they would have returned without gaining any information whatsoever. Personally, I am inclined to think that the latter would have been the case, and that they would never have pushed home their patrols with sufficient determination to be of any real use.

September and the first half of October passed without event, but on the 15th of the latter month a new force was formed which practically took the place of the old Derby and Notts Mounted Brigade. This force was placed under the command of Lieut.-Colonel Neilson, and was composed of the Derbyshire Yeomanry, two squadrons of Surrey Yeomanry (under Lieut.-Colonel Olive, M.C.), the Argyll Mountain Battery (Major Hicks, M.C.), and three companies of Cyclists (Major Green, M.C.). On the 24th the Regiment took over the duties of patrolling from the Surrey Yeomanry to the south and east of Osman Kamilla. It was considered that one troop of not less than twenty men with one Hotchkiss gun would be sufficient for the objects in view, namely, to keep the enemy's forward line under constant observation, and to locate all posts and wire; to estimate the strength of the enemy holding the forward posts by constant observation; and to study the course of the patrols sent out by the Bulgars.

BIG COMBINED MOVEMENT

On the following day, the Regiment took part in the biggest combined show which had come their way for

M

some time. Though this was not a complete success, it was, nevertheless, sufficiently so to justify a short description of the operation. It well exemplifies the difficulty which is always found in getting troops who do not know each other and have not previously worked together to combine together with the best results. I do not infer that there is ever the slightest lack of willingness, but other elements such as speed of movement come in which make co-operation and co-ordination lose much of its value. The Corps troops, namely, those which I have just mentioned, under Lieut.-Colonel Neilson crossed the Gudeli bridge at 11.30 at night in order to operate against Karakaska whilst working in conjunction with the 82nd Infantry Brigade, who were to operate against the line Salmak to Ada. The Argyll Mountain Battery did not participate. The operation, always a difficult one, consisted of a combined attack to be made by separate bodies of troops, who had to march by separate routes and converge on the objective. The Corps Cyclists who crossed the Gudeli bridge at 9.45 at night had orders to move well clear of the village of that name until they struck the Meander brook, which they were to follow to the south until it brought them to the Karakaska bridge. They were then to attack Karakaska in conjunction with the two squadrons of Surrey Yeomanry, plus " C " Squadron Derbyshire Yeomanry, all under the command of Lieut.-Colonel Olive. This latter force, on reaching Gudeli Wood, tied up their horses and marched dismounted via Komarju, where touch was to be made with the Cyclists, and the village of Karakaska attacked from the south and south-east at 6.10 a.m. Both forces were late, and those to arrive first were the Cyclists, who attacked on their own and entered the village, but only captured three prisoners. The enemy had evidently got wind of the proceedings, for they were reported by aeroplane to have retired in the direction of Pheasant Wood. The remaining two squadrons of the Regiment never had an opportunity of coming into action. Things went better on the right, however, as might be expected from troops who were well acquainted with one another, and the total day's bag amounted to the very respectable total of 107 prisoners and 60 killed. The Corps troops on this occasion lost one officer and one other ranks killed, and three other ranks wounded.

The Regiment maintained the usual routine of patrols until November 5th, when they were relieved by the Surrey Yeomanry.

SUCCESSFUL AMBUSCADE

On November 10th "A" and "C" Squadrons brought off a successful little ambuscade. On the previous evening, "C" Squadron, less one troop which was attached to "A," crossed the Gudeli bridge and moved, mounted, into Jemimah, whilst "A" Squadron, after tying up their horses in Gudeli Wood, moved, dismounted, to lie up and await any parties of the enemy coming into Karakaska in the early morning. About 7.30 a.m., sure enough, some sixty or seventy came along, and Lieutenant Wright's troop, which was covering the bridge, held their fire until the enemy's advanced points were almost on them. The other troops joined in almost simultaneously. For about ten minutes the Bulgars put up a fight without doing us any damage whatsoever, and then retired, leaving four dead and several wounded, and it is probable that these were not their only casualties or anything like it.

Two days later we again took over the patrolling from the Surrey Yeomanry.

Patrol schemes, however well thought out and cunningly laid, are apt to "gang agley." As an instance of this a capital little scheme was arranged on the 21st, and it was nobody's fault that no result was achieved. The Argyll Mountain Battery, with an escort of Cyclists, moved across the river so as to take up a position before dark. These were also accompanied by a section of 18-pounders (two guns). The following morning, Major Clark was despatched on the usual patrol with orders to approach Ada and endeavour to draw the enemy from there in the direction of a wood to the west side of Kispeki, when they would be dealt with by the artillery.   Everything, as arranged, went well, but unfortunately one all-important essential was absent—namely, the enemy!   It takes two to make a battle, and that this one should prove a wash-out was sheer bad luck, as the enemy could safely have been relied on to be present in these villages nine times out of ten or more.   In such patrol schemes, the worst of it is that if one fails, such as in this case, it is frequently not safe or wise to try and repeat the performance, as there is no knowing how much the enemy may have seen, or whether he has been able to put two and two together so as to make four.   Thus a good idea which does not fructuate is probably lost for good and all —at least in that locality.   Patrol work, to be successful, therefore requires constant change of system, together with much originality.

LARGER SCALE OPERATIONS

A variation of this last scheme, but on a considerably larger scale, was attempted a few days before Christmas. On this occasion four villages were reconnoitred, and the Derby and Surrey Yeomanry had orders, in the event of any two of them being strongly held, to gallop round to the north side, to dismount and attack on foot with bayonet and bomb, so as to drive out the enemy to the south and into the arms (no joke intended) of our infantry and artillery, who had moved up under cover and were waiting to receive the foe.

Once again, with the exception of twelve men in Karakaska, the enemy were conspicuous by their absence and the making of a very pretty little fight was spoiled.

The same operations were attempted on two later occasions, but in both cases the operation was cancelled owing to heavy rain on the 29th, and deep mud and consequent heavy going on January 2nd.

This at last brings us to 1918, the final year of the war. Doubtless the readers of this will be as glad as the men who were serving would have been could they have known it.

January proved to be a very quiet month, and not once did the Regiment get to grips with the Bulgars. The duties of the patrol line were taken alternately by the Derbyshire and Surrey Yeomanry. On February 9th, a review was held near Orljak for H.M. the King of Greece, the Regiment being represented on this occasion by one squadron and the machine-gun section, both under the command of Major Branfill.

Another successful little affray took place on the 27th. On this occasion " B " Squadron marched out at 11 p.m. on the night of the 26th, under the command of Major Johnson, and lay up in Beglimah to await the arrival of enemy patrols in the morning. About 8 a.m. a mounted patrol turned up and was heavily fired on at close range, with the result that five horses were seen to fall and none of their riders were seen to rise.

In March our forces commenced to swell, for the Greek army was now beginning to enter the field after their reorganisation and re-training, and on the 16th the First Greek Division commenced to concentrate at Nigoslav.

During what may be called the slack period of the winter, football and boxing tournaments were frequently held. In both of these the Regiment distinguished itself, and in the latter sport proved to be the possessor of a very useful bantam weight in Private Fletcher. Fletcher, after winning the Corps Novices competition, was eligible to compete in the Army and Navy Tournament, held at Lembet Camp, and so well did he acquit himself that he actually reached the final, and was only beaten on points by Private Scates of the 27th Division.

RUSSIANS AS FIGHTERS

Amongst the extraordinary assortment of races which we had fighting for us in Macedonia we numbered a contingent of Russians. These were at Saramanli, and owing to the upheaval in Russia announced that they were not prepared to fight any more (I am unaware that they had ever been particularly guilty in this respect !), but that they would work (?). This declaration was the means of giving Lieutenant Vaughan and his troop a most trying and thoroughly unpleasant march, for he was ordered to join them and assist them in their endeavours.. On the 27th he departed, and reached the forty-fourth kilometre stone on the way the same day. It had been snowing hard, with the result that it was impossible to ride, and the horses had to be led the whole way. Those who have led a horse on impossible roads covered with snow even for a short distance will realise what a forty-four kilo. march must have entailed. Having reached Gunesne on the 28th, he received orders to halt owing to the impossible weather conditions, and here he remained until April 1st (a most fitting day for such an errand), when he completed his march.

On April 6th the regimental football team, which had worked its way through the Corps League, reached the final, but was beaten 4—1 by the Cameron Highlanders. This may well be considered a fine performance for a mounted regiment, for not only were its numbers approximately half those of an infantry battalion, but, in addition, owing to constant patrolling by day, its opportunities of playing the whole team together were strictly limited.

On the same day a party of some twenty-five Bulgars got a bit of their own back by lying up in ambush at Hursley Park. Only our advanced section came under fire, but two men were wounded. One of these, Private White, was brought out of action by Sergeant J. W. Outram, who displayed great gallantry, and thoroughly deserved the Military Medal which the Corps Commander bestowed on him three days later.

FIRST GREEK OFFENSIVE

Things now commenced to assume a rather different aspect, and on the 15th the Greek army made their first offensive move by crossing the Struma by night and occupying the villages from Beglimah Wood to Ada, whilst our 27th Division prolonged their line to the left. Both these forces were guided up to their objectives by our men, and no casualties were sustained. The Greeks, however, did not hold this line for long, and retired to the south or right bank of the river on the 21st, leaving a detachment at Jemimah.

This operation may not sound much in itself, but it must be remembered that at this time things were looking distinctly murky in France, where the Boche had driven us practically to the outskirts of Amiens in the south of the British line, and had shortly afterwards driven in our line immediately north of Bethune and had created a deep salient which, extending north, had compelled us to evacuate the Passchendale ridge, which we had captured with such terrific loss, and were even now threatening a great attack with massed troops under Prince Ruprecht with the apparent intention of an immediate break through towards Cassel and the almost inevitable fall of Calais. Such being the case in France, one must suppose that our troops elsewhere would feel the reflection of the general depression, and would welcome to an exaggerated degree any fresh assistance to their fighting strength as well as any tendency towards an offensive.

Had they known it, the worst had been passed on all fronts, the Germans had almost exhausted themselves, and the tide of victory, though hardly noticeable, had already turned.

About this time a despatch-riding competition for officers was held, and in this the Derbyshire Yeomanry were well represented, for in the light-weights, Captain Jackson was first and Major Johnson second, whilst Lieutenant Lowe was second in the heavy-weight race.

After the 27th a new system of patrolling was instituted, and mixed patrols consisting of a troop of Yeomanry and a platoon of Cyclists were in future utilised. This was nothing new or original, for both the Germans and Bulgars had constantly used such mixed patrols ever since we had first arrived in Macedonia.

All remained comparatively quiet during the rest of April and for the whole of May, about the middle of which month the Greeks took over the patrolling from us and the Surrey Yeomanry for two days in each week, namely, Mondays and Thursdays, which was naturally a great relief to the regiments concerned.

At this time the Regiment was well up to strength, and numbered 28 officers and 578 other ranks.

On June 7th Lieutenant Vaughan and his troop returned from the Russians at Saramanli, and during the whole of the month the usual routine of patrolling was continued without any further change of line.

On July 1st Lieutenant Calder, who had done excellent work as transport officer ever since leaving Egypt in February, 1916, left the Regiment *en route* for India to join the reserve of Officers, Indian Army. Everyone regretted his departure.

A SUDDEN CHANGE

On July 12th affairs took a sudden change for the Regiment, for it received orders to move to Sarigol, which is close to Kukus and immediately behind its old friend the Gola Ridge. The move was commenced by " A " Squadron on the following day, each of the other squadrons following at intervals of a day, and, marching via Lahana, concentrated at Sarigol on the 17th.

Two days later the 16th Corps Cyclists joined the Regiment, and at the same time the Surrey Yeomanry were withdrawn to Lahana. A move of this description always makes speculation rife, but on this occasion, though rumours of an advance were thick in the air, nothing eventuated—the Regiment once again took up the routine of training, and to everyone's joy a limited amount of leave was given ; those who were not fortunate enough to obtain leave in England were granted short leave to Salonica. Even this was better than nothing, and to get one's nose into a real glass containing something cool and strong, to sit down to a very moderate dinner which seemed a feast, and to find oneself in a real bed, must have indeed been a novelty.

I think that during our occupation of Macedonia, Salonica must have become one of the rich cities of the world ! It is certain that by the time any British soldier arrived there his money was burning a hole in his pocket, and it is equally certain that the Greeks, Spaniards, Turks and Jews who chiefly went to make up its citizenship were " no slouches " in extracting the same. Salonica had few attractions other than architectural, but those few were thoroughly well organised. Who will not remember the " Leicester Lounge," or be forgetful of the " Odéon " ?

Not that the latter was expensive to get into, but it had a knack of proving itself so afterwards, and before one's egress was effected. As I remember it, the chief cause of this unexpected expenditure was a so-called " Spanish dancer." I doubt her being Spanish, but have no doubts about her being unable to dance. At a distance, and on the stage, she appeared to be attractive—this, and the construction of the Odéon, led to the undoing of possibly thousands. The Odéon, a small theatre or music hall, comprised a horse-shoe of minute boxes, tier upon tier, whilst the auditorium—a misnomer in this case—was packed with little tables surrounded by French, Greek, Italian and Servian officers and men, and surmounted with a plentiful array of bottles and glasses. The British mostly retained the boxes.

What, then, was one's joy, having witnessed the evolutions of the fair Spaniard, when an attendant announced her arrival at your box door ? The following

illuminating conversation would then take place, and
it must have been almost verbatim throughout the
war. " Bon soit, Mademoiselle, parlez vous Anglais ? "
" Bon soit, Messieurs, non." " Parlez vous Francais ? "
" Pas de tout." " Voulez vous avez de champagne ? "
" Oui." " Boy, Champagne ! " Instantaneous arrival
of boy and forty-five drachmae is demanded for a bottle
of very doubtful origin. " Votre santé, Mademoiselle."
" Votre santé, Messieurs." (Conversation flags, and
everyone else asks if anyone speaks any Spanish.)
We drink our champagne—the fair Spaniard leaves her
glass untasted. An awkward pause, broken, to everyone's relief, by the entry of an attendant bearing a
tray full of chocolates. " Ah, les chocolates ! "—this
from Mademoiselle. Much money changes hands ;
Mademoiselle's lap is heaped with boxes which remain
unopened. Another awkward pause, which is again
relieved at the exact moment by the tactful entry of
the same attendant, this time bearing a tray containing
bunches of violets. Again Mademoiselle is first off
the mark with " Ah, les violets ! " and again we vie
with one another in our generosity. After a short
pause, Mademoiselle will now exclaim, " Voila, mes
amis," pointing to a box opposite, and will murmur
" Un moment," and therewith take her departure,
leaving you speculating as to whether you have created
the right impression. You have. You will look with
jealous eyes towards the other box, and gradually it
will dawn upon you that " you've been had," for you
will see identically the same little play reacted ; nay,
more, you will almost hear the successive cries of
pleased surprise : " Le champagne, les chocolates, les
violets." Further, you will probably notice, with your
eye well trained through constant patrol work, that
though Mademoiselle left you with her lap full of the
two latter commodities, she has entered the opposite
box with that receptacle empty. You will realise,
with a brain wave, that the identical articles are once
again changing hands, and before you have fully grasped

the horror of the situation, your box door will open, and, before you have realised it, there is the " beautiful " Spaniard with an " Ah, mes amis " given with an air of fatigue (and the poor thing probably is so, for she has wasted little time), to be immediately followed by a small gasp, a patting of the throat, and a murmur (you have probably guessed it) of " Encore du champagne." This time we firmly say " Non, non," and she leaves the box in a well-assumed huff. Almost immediately a scuffling is heard next door, and we climb up and peer over the partition of the adjoining box. Here we see " Cardinal Wiseman " in the shape of a gunner subaltern, who has not only heard, but has used his ears and eyes to good effect. His position is undignified, but eminently suited to the occasion. He is obviously a student of minor tactics. He is sitting on the floor—his back is to the door—his feet braced against the front of the box, and he is putting out herculean efforts. Though the door bends, it does not yield. We hear a murmur which sounds like " cochon "—the subaltern looks up and grins, and we find it in our hearts to congratulate him.

I need say nothing about the " Leicester Lounge " except that its habitués declared, nay, boasted almost, that there is no place in Salonica where money lasted such a short time ! I believe that the boast was no vain one.

CHAPTER XIII

SALONICA—*continued*

THANKS TO THE REGIMENT

SOON after the Regiment arrived at Sarigol the following letter was received. It speaks for itself. Readers of this narrative may judge for themselves whether it was well deserved or not.

Letter received from 16th Corps :—

O.C., 1/1st Derbyshire Yeomanry.

On the departure of the Derbyshire Yeomanry from the 16th Corps, General Briggs wishes to thank Lieut.-Colonel Neilson D.S.O., and Officers, N.C.O.'s, and men for the excellent work they have done for him during the period they have served under his command. The zeal, fighting spirit, and sound patrol methods of the Regiment have always evoked his pleasure and admiration.

He wishes them every possible good luck, and hopes that if ever an advance takes place on this front that they may again come under his command.

(Signed) E. D. YOUNG,
Brigadier-General,
July 19th, 1918.   D.A. & Q.M.G.

On August 2nd, Captain B. H. G. Arkwright, who for some time had been Adjutant of the Regiment, and who had done good work since the commencement of the war, not only with it but in transport duties at Alexandria, to which service he was attached, on the appointment of the Regiment, for a considerable time, left for England on leave, and the duties of Adjutant were taken over by Lieutenant W. J. Blanksby, who had served with the Regiment in Gallipoli as a sergeant and thereafter had gained his commission.

As August drew to a close rumour became more and more insistent that an advance was shortly to be made, not a partial one this time, but a grand affair in which the French, Serbs, the Greeks and ourselves were all to co-operate to our fullest strength.

With September came obvious indications that rumour for once had not lied, though nothing was definitely known as to the probable date. When orders do come on such occasions they have the habit of coming suddenly and unexpectedly ; and this occasion proved to be no exception to the rule. September 16th found the Regiment still at Sarigol, and that afternoon orders to move to Alexia suddenly arrived. The orders were urgent, and by 7 p.m. tents had been struck, everything had been packed, and the Regiment was once more on the move.

Unfortunately, the Regiment at this time was in a weak state, for, as usual, malaria had been at work during the summer months, with the result that a great many men were now in hospital. In addition to this, a number of both officers and men were on leave in England, thus depleting the strength still further.

The Regiment marched out under Colonel Neilson, with Major Tremayne as second-in-command, and the squadrons were commanded as follows : " A " Squadron, Major Branfill; " B " Squadron, Captain Jackson ; and " C " Squadron, Major Birchenough, to whom I am indebted for much of the information which goes to make up the subsequent history. Lieutenant Blanksby was Adjutant, and Captain Huddy the Medical Officer. The ranks were so depleted that " C " Squadron, for instance, marched out of camp at barely half strength, or, to be accurate, with four officers and seventy-eight N.C.O.'s and other ranks.

Alexia was reached by a march during that night, and a troublesome march it was, owing to the constant slipping of packs. These things will happen in the best regulated of families, and the tendency for packs to slip is greatly increased when a regiment has been at rest for some time, and horses and mules, which were formerly hard and lean, have been steadily putting on flesh.

All that day the Regiment lay concealed in a gully near Alexia, so as to escape observation (for the attack had not yet been opened, and it was essential that all the opening movements should pass unobserved), and moved that night to Piton Gallieni.

Piton Gallieni is almost due south of Doiran, and on reaching here Headquarters, together with "B" Squadron and the M.G. section, moved on to Waring's Bridge, which was the name given to the bridge over the stream below Colonial Hill (so called from its having been occupied and held by the French Colonial Division). They were thus in a position and in readiness to move and to push through any gap which should be formed in the event of a successful attack.

THE LIE OF THE LAND

Before proceeding further it will be as well, for the benefit of readers who know not the country, to give a very brief description of the general lie of the land, and also of the approximate position of the Allied forces.

I have already described Lake Doiran and the country overlooking it both from our side, namely, the Gola Ridge, and also from the Bulgar positions on the Belashitza mountains to the north of the intervening plain.

Opposite the ridge the plain is a good seven miles in width, which, apart from the impregnable heights on the north side, was sufficient in itself to preclude a successful surprise attack. At the west end of both the ridge and the plain and on the far side of and parallel to the Kilindir river, which flows due south out of Lake Doiran, ran a spur of hills, already mentioned, cut up on the side towards the river by several deep ravines. This ridge was held by the enemy, and covered all approaches towards Doiran town and the main road from it to the north. From a point near Kilindir this formation of hills curved south-west, and overlooked the plateau which extended northwards from Kukus to Kilindir, and which was bounded on the west by Lake Ardzan—in fact, it formed the rim of a saucer.

The hills held by the enemy thus formed a salient overlooking plains on its two sides (one plain being higher than the other), which plains were separated by the Gola Ridge, which met the salient roughly at its apex.

It was the lot of the British 12th Corps and the Greeks, who were acting in close co-operation, to attack this mountainous salient from its two sides, and so to force a way to Doiran. I will omit the part played by the French as their action in no way concerned the part which the Regiment played in the advance.

The fourth army of the Allies was that of the Serbians, who were placed on our left (*i.e.*, the west) of our line. Their front lay opposite the river Vardar, which ran north and south through the enemy's and their lines. The mountains west of this river were of a precipitous nature, and were all held by the enemy. The crossing of this river in itself was an almost insuperable difficulty, and this left, as the only possible means of advance, the sector which lay between the left, or west, of the salient I have just mentioned, and the point where the river passed through the Bulgar lines somewhere near Smol. It was on this front then that the Serbian attack was made.

That the attack was successful is a glorious page in the history of Serbia. Faced with steep mountains, which had been made practically impregnable by every art of engineering known to the German engineers attached to the Bulgars, failure would have been no disgrace to even the finest troops in the world. I believe that without the bitter hatred for the devastators of their country, together with the very real spirit of patriotism and the determination of every man to win or die for his country, the thing would have been impossible.

THE ADVANCE BEGINS

At dawn on September 18th the British and Greeks attacked. The battle lasted all day, and both sides suffered heavy losses. This was especially so in the case of the British, to whose lot it fell to attack the

Pips, a group of high conical hills rather behind the apex of the angle to which I have referred. This attack was carried out by the 12th Corps, whose losses were very heavy, a great proportion of which were sustained in the deep gullies or ravines which intersected the hills. The Bulgar positions were of the strongest possible nature, and were strengthened by many well concealed and equally well-placed machine-gun positions. Both of these attacks failed, as in spite of gallant attempts no break through was effected. In consequence of this, Headquarters and " B " Squadron returned to Piton Gallieni after nightfall, and here rejoined the rest of the Regiment. Though the fighting was resumed the following day, very little further progress was made, which resulted in the Regiment receiving orders that evening to return to its old camp at Sarigol, marching via Hadzi-Janis and Armutci. The Regiment moved at 10 o'clock that night, and reached Sarigol at 3.30 on the morning of the 20th. Before leaving Sarigol on the 16th, tents had been struck and everything packed up and the whole business of pitching camp had in consequence to be gone through again, as information had been received that there was no likelihood of the Regiment being required.

On the very next day, the 21st, to everyone's joy, the news came through that the Serbians had been successful in their attack, and had not merely broken through but that they were " fairly hunting " the Bulgars, to use the expression of an eye-witness, and within a very few hours an order arrived for the Regiment to move at once. The Regiment had only been in camp for less than twenty-four hours, but nobody minded that, for the new order was for the Vardar front, and by 8.30 the same evening the Regiment (23 officers and 358 other ranks, with 374 horses and 164 mules) was off, and, after a night march, arrived on the west side of Lake Ardzan at 2.45 next morning. By 8 a.m. they were off again, and by noon had reached the Grey Rocks, where a most welcome stream was found, for

CAPTAIN F. B. SWANWICK

Adjutant of the Regiment from 1915

by this time everyone, both men and horses, were coated with dust both inside and out.

AFTER THE BULGARS

Here the night was spent, but by 5 a.m. the Regiment was on the march, with orders to find the Bulgars as the infantry had lost touch—a very different state of affairs to the wearisome years of never ceasing patrolling in front of an enemy's position which never changed. Within a few miles the Regiment marched through what had, a couple of days before, been the enemy's front line, thence through the villages of Stojakovo and Bogdanci. Everywhere there were signs of Bulgars, and what was the most important, ample evidence of a hurried retreat, for on every hand were to be seen arms and ammunition boxes, dead men and broken wagons, limbers with their dead teams and canteen stores—all the desolate-looking remnants of a beaten army. There is always something depressing about the leavings of a retreating army, even if it's that of the enemy. I suppose it's the loss of discipline and the break up of the organisation which has taken so long to build up. For all that, it has, at the same time, a wonderfully heartening effect!

Leaving Bogdanci the Regiment moved up the Furka Dere, taking all due precautions, as no one could foretell where the Bulgar rear-guard might put up a fight. Even so our advance guard bumped into them rather suddenly. "C" Squadron were acting as advance guard on this occasion, and, unknown to them, the Bulgars were holding a ridge near the head of the Dere (in this case a ravine with a dry river bed at the bottom) with their rear-guard, supported by machine and mountain guns. The latter allowed the advanced troop of the squadron to "make good" a small hill without molestation, and then suddenly opened a heavy artillery fire on the rest of the squadron, which was now coming up to take over the hill preparatory to making the next "bound" forward.

N

Not much damage was done, and fortunately the squadron managed to find a way to the top of the hill, where their advanced troop was isolated and thus render them necessary support. After hiding the horses in a convenient gully, nothing remained but to sit tight, and this they did, spending a most uncomfortable afternoon, as the hill was overlooked by that held by the Bulgars, who made use of this to spray it periodically with machine-gun fire.

This sort of fight is poor fun at the best, and it is not improved by a hot sun and an entire absence of water. Can it be wondered at that thoughts turned to the Bulgar canteen stores which had been left behind at Bogdanci with much regret !

The situation was relieved with the approach of evening as the advance guard of the Greeks came up, and to them was handed over the clearing up of the situation, leaving the Regiment to go into bivouac for the night north-west of Furka.   During this engagement the Regiment itself had also been shelled, and it subsequently transpired, through the few inhabitants, that the Bulgars had left behind a force of 300 infantry with nine guns to hold it up.

ON AGAIN AT DAWN

At dawn on the 24th the hunt was again taken up, with " B " Squadron in advance, with orders to patrol the villages of Dedeli, Cestovo, Tartali, Rabrovo, and Vallandovo.   All the villages proved to be unoccupied, with the exception of Vallandovo, whence a few Bulgars retreated and retired to the hills, and the Regiment streamed over the plain between Cestovo and Vallandovo in great style after a terribly hot time climbing down ravines and up the other side, for the only road was under shell fire, and to have taken it would have meant needless casualties.   During this march Colonel Neilson displayed a great " eye for the country," and it was owing to his skilful guidance that only one casualty was sustained up to this point, namely, Lieutenant H. E. Gillett, who was wounded.

Piravo was patrolled by " A " Squadron, who found it unoccupied by the enemy, who had left behind a hospital full of our wounded prisoners, who had been captured in the fighting on the 18th, when the British made their attack on Doiran. It is easy to picture the joy of these men on finding themselves again free in less than a week, and to know that their efforts had not been in vain.

At Piravo there was every sign of a hurried flight. During the afternoon touch was again established with the enemy, who held the Regiment up amongst the foothills near Tartali, and here the two squadrons (" A " and " C "), with Headquarters, found cover in a river bed, from whence they engaged the Bulgars for the remainder of the day, until the Greeks again came up and were duly handed over the control of affairs. This allowed the Regiment to retire a short distance and go into bivouac for a much-needed and well-earned rest. During the afternoon Staff-Sergeant-Major Gillott and Private Bryan were wounded by shell fire. The loss of Staff-Sergeant-Major Gillott, especially at this juncture, was a great blow to " C " Squadron.

The Greeks, left to their own devices, wisely waited until dark, when they went for the Bulgar, and again put him to flight.

HEREDITARY FOES AT GRIPS

I should have been very sorry to have been a Bulgar in those days, and to have found a victorious Greek army up against me, and I doubt whether I should have stood my ground very long. The hatred which the Macedonian Greeks had for the Bulgars, their hereditary enemies, was intense. It was a real and vivid thing with them, and quite unlike any hatred which I have met elsewhere. One had only to see the countless Greek villages which had been absolutely wiped out in previous wars, and to hear the numerous tales of children being butchered by having their brains dashed out against the walls of their homes to realise

this, and to understand that a victorious Greek, with
his blood thoroughly up, was no sort of a person to meet
face to face at the right end of a bayonet on a dark
night! I fancy that when, on such occasions, the
Bulgars did go, they " went *some*," to use the language
of the States.

On the morning of the 25th the chase was once more
resumed, and this time " A " Squadron led the way.
The only road through the hills was under shell fire,
and therefore to be avoided, and " A " Squadron,
working up a ravine to the east of the Dedeli-Kosturino
road, and moving by way of Kajahli, and round the
Dorsale-des-Arbres, which left Kosturino to their
right or east, occupied the high ground at Conevert de
Cepelli Piton, where they were later joined by " C "
Squadron.

This march was very rough, consisting as it did of
a series of gullies, and one of these was particularly
beastly, for in it our aeroplanes had caught the Bulgar
transport, and you can picture what that means!
You can imagine the road first of all blocked in front,
and then an aeroplane armed with bombs and machine
guns sailing low over a struggling mass of men and
maddened horses, and, believe me, that gully could
have been no nice place to have passed through on a
hot day. Perhaps they were not so badly off as our
artillery, who had to traverse the main road, for along
this the stench was so dreadful in places that the men
had to put on their gas masks.

On this ridge the two squadrons were shelled in-
effectively from the road leading to Popcevo, and were
also troubled from the fire of two machine guns from
somewhere in the neighbourhood of Lake Ecran.

GOING LIKE CLOCKWORK

After pushing in the Bulgar rearguard, Kosturino
was reached and passed (here the Commanding Officer
of " C " Squadron had to leave a very tempting "dump,"
much to his regret), but after progressing a little further

the usual thing happened, for at about 3 p.m. the rear-guard were again encountered, holding on to the usual ridge, and supported by well-placed machine-guns. All efforts to dislodge them being without avail, the Regiment went into bivouac near Kosturino. The Greeks had arrived with nightfall, and again took over proceedings—in fact, the whole thing was going like clockwork, and almost as if it had been pre-arranged.

Men and horses were by now feeling the strain of the constant heat, the continual scrambling over rough ground, and the daily spells of fighting and almost incessant shelling. Water was what was needed more than anything.

During the afternoon the advance squadrons had an annoying experience, for though themselves held by the enemy's rear-guard, they were still able to see their main body streaming away over the ridge beyond. It was useless to put up prayers for horse artillery or mountain guns, for they were miles beyond our ken; nevertheless, if they had been there they would have had the chance of a lifetime—or so the advanced squadrons opined. During the day Privates Lloyd, Gladwyn and Palmer were wounded.

September 26th proved to be a most eventful day, for it showed that operations were about to culminate in a grand finale. As usual, the Regiment was up " bright and early " (perhaps more of the latter than the former), and the Greeks having successfully completed their share of fighting during the night and reporting " All clear," the Regiment moved off before dawn.

THE KEY TO BULGARIA

The object on this day was to reach the all-important Strumitza Valley, the key to Bulgaria, and success was of vital importance. The Regiment was at this time separated from the valley by a chain of steep mountains through which only two roads gave access to the valley below.

It was decided, as information as to the enemy's positions and intentions were meagre, to attempt the passage by both roads. " C " Squadron was on the roster this day for advance guard, and was accordingly despatched under Major Birchenough by one road with orders to get to Strumitza at all costs. The remainder of the Regiment, with " B " Squadron in advance, took the other road.

" C " Squadron had a nasty job in front of them, for they soon found that the road ran between precipitous walls of rock which allowed of progression by the road alone and put flank guards out of the question. The only possible course was to push on as speedily as possible, and this they did, expecting to meet the Bulgar, and to find themselves in a trap, at every corner. After progressing for about two miles, the other road to the west was sighted, and, moreover, " B " Squadron was seen to be on it.

Here quite a dramatic incident occurred, for as " C " Squadron were taking in the situation they saw a cloud of dust rapidly approaching " B " Squadron, and as this slowed down it transformed itself into a motor car bearing a large white flag—the preliminaries to the Bulgar surrender. Major Birchenough helioed over to Regimental Headquarters with " B " Squadron to ask " what was up," and was told that the Bulgars wanted peace, but that he was to push on as hard as possible.

Finding that Greek infantry or " feet " were hard at their heels, and going strong with their tails well up, no time was lost and the advance was resumed. After pushing on, numerous Bulgar peasants began to be met with, and as these were almost paralytic from fear, and apparently expected to be killed and eaten, Peter Pericles (the squadron interpreter) was in great demand. He not only restored their confidence and made them happy, but what was of far greater importance, actually collected some eggs from them. Information was obtained from the peasants that the Bulgars were beyond Strumitza. The squadron was now getting on fast, but the victorious Greeks were still pressing hard on their heels, and, as it looked like a regular race for the honour of reaching this vital point, Major Birchenough took Lieutenant Domleo's troop, and leaving the rest of the squadron under Captain Swanwick, pushed on quickly and galloped down into the plain. The squadron followed in great style, and sent on another troop to go round the town whilst Major Birchenough entered it.

No Bulgars were found within a mile, and the only hostiles encountered were seven Huns who were found sitting disconsolately on their baggage waiting for transport—these were taken prisoners.

ENTRY INTO STRUMITZA

Shortly afterwards " B " Squadron arrived by the other road, and according to orders pushed on. " C " Squadron's entry into Strumitza was most dramatic. To quote Major Birchenough's own words : " Apparently they took me for their deliverer. The church bells rang, and we (both men and horses) were decorated with flowers. Luckily many were scented geraniums, as the smell of dead animals was too awful. They wanted me to receive the Mayor and Corporation, and to receive the keys of the city and to attend service in the church. Not having time, I said that the Colonel was the man for that."

" B " Squadron had now got into touch with the enemy, and the remainder of the Regiment had come up. The Bulgars now commenced to throw over some shells, and cover became essential. Fortunately, there was a slight fog in the valley, which allowed the Regiment to be moved into the maize fields and mulberry groves, which surrounded the town, unobserved. The enemy continued to shell all the afternoon, and concentrated on the roads leading into the plain, with the result that our transport, who were following along behind, came in for a nasty time of it, and suffered some casualties.

Both the heat and dust had been very trying all day, and, as can be imagined, men and horses had had enough of it and were thankful to get into bivouac.

Next day, the 27th, the same old story was repeated, and the Regiment again found itself on the move before dawn. The poor old horses were about played out, and so, indeed, were the men, but both played up splendidly. Important movements were now in progress. According to programme, the direction of the advance was now changed to east. With " A " Squadron as advance guard, the Regiment now moved off down the valley towards Petric with the object of cutting off the Bulgar retreat from the Struma Valley via the Rupel Pass, their only exit.

All day the hills on either side of the valley were covered in mist, which may account for the fact that with the exception of a few hostile patrols, who retired on our advance, no enemy were encountered and nothing was done to bar the advance.

A halt for the night was made at Bosiljovo.

Though the inhabitants of the villages through which the Regiment passed were suspicious of what the British would do to them, and naturally so, after their frequent experiences in former Balkan wars, the population as a whole were delighted to see our men. Every house had a white flag up, and everywhere the Regiment was met with " peace offerings " of a most acceptable nature, namely, bread and fried eggs. Under these circumstances our men were not slow in fraternising. The only fly in the ointment was the difficulty of consuming the said " peace offerings," and as the men rode along their tunics bore witness to this.

Water was now more plentiful—a great blessing, as the horses had had to go short for days on end.

A battery of field artillery was now attached to the Regiment.

On that memorable night at Bosiljovo fresh mutton appeared for dinner—history does not relate where it was obtained. In connection with this I should here like to pay a well-deserved tribute to the cooks of the Regiment. No praise can be too great for them, and to their efforts is largely due the fact that the men kept going during this long and trying advance. Whenever a halt was made, something was ready for all ranks. When camp was made late at night the cooks were the last to go to bed—before dawn, day after day, the Regiment was on the march, and the cooks had to be the first up. They had less rest than anyone. It is an open question whether they ever had any sleep at all!

" UNCONDITIONAL SURRENDER "

During the evening more peace envoys passed through and the Regiment learned that our terms were those of " unconditional surrender."

Before daylight on the 28th the Regiment, with " B " Squadron in advance, was well upon its way to Jenikoi. Here the valley became very narrow, and with the hills on both sides, formed a regular bottle-neck, and here " B " Squadron found the Bulgars. Supporting their infantry were one or two batteries of field artillery, which opened fire and rather took us by surprise.

The Regiment opened out and wheeled to a flank as if on parade, whilst its accompanying battery, who had kept rather too closely up, had to turn and gallop for it and had one limber smashed up by shell fire.

By the time the enemy's flanks had been located and were proved to be resting on the hills on either side of the valley, it was dusk, and the Greeks having now come up, the situation was handed over to them, and the Regiment allowed to go into bivouac at Borihovo.

More envoys came through, but what was of far greater importance, rations, for the first time during the advance, failed to turn up, and the Regiment became dependent on local supplies. As these supplies took the form of fresh mutton and eggs for the men, and barley and hay for the horses, nobody found it in their hearts to hurl anathema at the delinquents.

Before dawn on the following day " C " Squadron moved off to establish touch with the enemy, and this was done just as it was getting light. Just as this was done, the Greeks made their attack, which caused the Bulgars to disclose the fact that they had a number of machine-guns and several batteries in position.

This put the squadron in a most uncomfortable position, for they found themselves in between the Bulgars and the barrage which they had put up against the Greeks, and which was gradually shortening and drawing nearer to the squadron as the Greeks advanced— which they did most gallantly and in short rushes. At this critical juncture the squadron was recalled, and was enabled to watch the battle from a safe distance. The Bulgars held on, and the battle lasted throughout the day. Though in the afternoon we brought up some " heavies," neither they nor the field artillery were able to locate the position of the Bulgar guns. During these operations one of our field batteries galloped into position in the open in a most gallant fashion, and came in for a very hot time.

TRIBUTE TO GALLANT GREEKS

Special mention must be made of the Greek 13th Division (with whom the Regiment was co-operating). Both here, as at Furka on the 23rd and at Tartali on the 24th of September, they behaved most gallantly, and well earned the admiration of all. Nothing stopped them. No matter how steep the hills, they rushed up them carrying their machine-guns. With less deter- mined troops the great success of these operations might well have never been achieved.

That night, at Borihovo, where bivouac was again made, the cooks offered up fresh pork for supper—the situation was rapidly improving !

In spite of no advance, both men and horses had had a very hard day, and were about played out.

Violent thunderstorms in the afternoon, which not only soaked them through and through, but left no dry spots on which a man could sleep, had not improved matters, but there was not a word of grumbling to be heard. On September 30th the grand finale was reached.

The Regiment had paraded before dawn, as had become usual, and were just about to move off, when orders to " stand fast " arrived. No one dared to hope, and few dared to believe, when a report came through that an armistice had been declared. Though this rumour was soon officially confirmed, no one much cared, in comparison to the fact that at last they could have a good day's rest, and even better still—a wash.

DECLARATION OF PEACE

October 1st.—Peace was officially declared, and the war and fighting, so far as concerned the Derbyshire Yeomanry, was at an end.

To celebrate the occasion, history relates that Captain Swanwick went out and bought two sheep, and, according to a diary, " we had such a dinner."

The Regimental Orders of the day contained the following :—

No. 1.—Peace with Bulgaria has been declared. The possessions of all inhabitants will be respected.

No. 2.—The following has been received from the 14th Hellenic Division, and is published for information :

I have the honour to request you to be so good as to express my thanks, and those of my Division, to the brave and able British artillery, which, by its splendid support, always assured the safe advance of my infantry.

My best thanks are also due to the 26th Division, which, in spite of tremendous difficulties, managed to keep us supplied with everything ; to the Field Ambulance, which showed wonderful devotion and ability in getting our wounded dressed and sent through to the base ; and to the Derbyshire Yeomanry, who kept us throughout perfectly informed and protected our flanks on two occasions.

I express to the G.O.C., 16th Corps, my joy at having contributed to the common victory under British orders. British command has, before now, proved its excellent influence on our troops, and we are and will be eternally grateful for all it has and is doing for us.

(Signed) JOHN H. ARPHARIDES.

October 2nd.—Regimental Order No. 1 :—

The Commanding Officer wishes to express his appreciation of the good work done by all ranks of the Regiment during the past fourteen days. The discipline and steadiness in the ranks has been exemplary, and has been largely responsible for the few casualties suffered.

The Corps Commander has personally remarked upon the Regiment's work, and has written to congratulate them upon what they have done.

I will quote one more order, namely, a Special Order of the day, received on the 11th, from General G. F. Milne, K.C.B., D.S.O., Commander-in-Chief British Salonica Force :—

Thanks to your gallantry, determination and devotion to duty, the Bulgarian army is now defeated, and the Bulgarian nation has sued for peace. This result has been obtained only by your extraordinary exertions after three summers spent in a malarious country and against obstacles of great natural and artificial strength. What appeared almost impossible has been accomplished. I gratefully thank you all, of every arm and of every rank, for your steadfast loyalty, your perfect discipline, and for the magnificent manner you have answered to every call made on you. No one knows better the odds against which you have had to contend, and I am proud to have had the honour of commanding you.

No more need be said, and no word of mine can add one particle to the name and achievement of the Regiment.

Since April, 1915, the Regiment had travelled thousands of miles, it had fought on many fronts, had undergone sickness and privation, had experienced intense heat and bitter cold, and had emerged at the end of nearly four years with not only an absolutely clean escutcheon, but with many laurels added to its name.

I hope that one day the deeds of our " Citizen Soldiers " may be more fully realised and better appreciated than they are now.

After Bulgaria had sued for peace, it was destined that the Regiment should take no further part in fighting during the remainder of the war, to the end of which our victory over the Bulgars was the prelude.

Though fighting was at an end for the Regiment, they had still much hard work in front of them, short rations for men and animals, horrible weather, and much work combined with long marches.

Before bringing this history to an end, it is well worth while briefly to outline these latter experiences. Those at home are apt to visualise the Tommy, the moment the last shot has been fired, as an emancipated person, so to speak, free from further responsibilities and duties and going about the conquered country as a light-hearted victor. They are far from the truth.

To resume. The termination of the fighting found the Regiment at Borihovo, and here they remained till the 5th. Though these five days were of comparative rest for the horses, they were days of great discomfort for the men. A cold rain descended incessantly, no overhead cover was available, and everyone was soaked through and through. To make matters worse, rations were coming up very irregularly. Orders were given to scour the country and make lists of all available supplies, more especially of hay. The latter commodity was a great problem, as horses were on very short rations, and the difficulty of obtaining it locally was greatly increased from the fact that the natives regarded it as of quite as much value as gold coinage, and, in fact, treated it as such by hiding it under the thatch of their roofs and in other inaccessible places, which made a census almost impossible. Lists of food supplies and of timber had also to be made, as the men were now on half rations. This necessarily entailed much work for all.

Rumours came through that Bulgaria had entirely " chucked it," but that Germany was sending troops to compel her again to take up arms and resume the fighting. There is no doubt that Germany did contemplate this, but were prevented from carrying it out owing to events on the Western front.

GRECO-BULGAR ENMITY

The Greeks and Bulgars were still ready to be at one another's throats, and the Regiment had to maintain a picket between the two opposing forces at Jenikoi to preserve law and order.

On October 6th the Regiment received orders to march to Petric, and moved off at 9 a.m. There is not usually much of value left behind in the camp of any Regiment which has had four years of active service, and, in this case, there could have been nothing owing to the shortage of rations. Nevertheless, as the Regiment marched out of camp there was a rush of the whole population of Borihovo to "loot" the leavings. The country had been so exhausted that the smallest thing, however useless, was of considerable value.

On its march the Regiment passed two Brigades of infantry, one of Greeks and one of Bulgars, the latter, a fine set of men compared with the Greeks, who are small and wiry, on their way to Petric to demobilise. Shortly afterwards the line of march took the Regiment through the last of the Bulgarian's main line of defences. This appeared to be well constructed and very strong in well and cunningly prepared artillery and machine-gun emplacements. Had they not given in when they did this line might well have proved a very serious obstacle to our further advance.

On reaching a point two miles south of Petric, the Regiment went into bivouac for the night, and a most uncomfortable one it proved to be, for not only did it rain all night, but the transport did not materialise until ten o'clock at night. Here the Regiment remained till the 9th, wet through all the time, short of rations, practically without hay, and, what was worst of all, from the men's point of view, totally without tobacco or cigarettes. Fortunately on the afternoon of the 8th, an enterprising Bulgar made his way into camp with a donkey load of the latter commodity, and, as you can imagine, did a roaring trade. Throughout Macedonia a donkey load *is* a donkey load. Though you can see the load a mile away the donkey remains absolutely invisible even at the closest quarters. If a Macedonian donkey were as big as a Shire horse he would carry England on his back.

THE MARCH RESUMED

The march towards Sofia was resumed on the 9th, and the passing of the Regiment through Petric, a most squalid place, caused considerable interest to the inhabitants and demobilised troops, of which the place was full. An amusing incident occurred here, for out of a hovel rushed a small and half-naked boy with a violin, who commenced playing the valse out of "The Merry Widow."

After another wet day, the Regiment went into bivouac at Orman, having covered fifteen miles. Fortunately, the night was fine, and the following morning, just as the troops were about to move, orders " to stand fast " arrived, and with them arrived the sun, which had not put in an appearance for many days. In spite of a shortage of rations, everyone was thoroughly happy, and the day was spent in drying clothes, or attempting to do so.

Next day the order of march was once more counter-ordered, and hard on the heels of the order came the rumour which declared that the Regiment was to become part of a flying column which was going to advance into Austria by way of Serbia.

Rumour was right in so far as it stated that the Regiment was not to take part in the triumphal march to Sofia, and next day they had the mortification of seeing an infantry brigade pass by *en route* for that place. The same evening, in the middle of tea to be precise, sudden orders arrived ordering the Regiment back to Orljak, on the south of the Struma, a place which has frequently been mentioned before.

This place was reached on the 13th, after an interesting but trying march—trying in that the rain still continued steadily ; interesting as the road took the Regiment through the famous Rupel Pass, the gateway into Bulgaria. It was curious that they should move through this from north to south, that is, from out of Bulgaria into Greece, for only three short weeks before it had been barring all advance from south to north. I fancy that everyone had expected to find enormously strong Bulgar defences guarding the Southern entrance to the pass, but as it turned out, these were conspicuous by their absence—a few gun positions and an incomplete Decauville railway were practically the only signs of their military occupation.

FORMIDABLE DEFENCES

After passing through Dermirhissar, where the bridge destroyed by the French at the beginning of 1916 was now being repaired, the Bulgar lines to the south of the town were crossed. These proved to be very formidable, and were of the greatest interest to all ranks, who had watched them for so long from the opposite direction, and who had carried out so many patrols in front of them.

Bivouac on October 12th was made at Ormanli, a place where we had had many patrol skirmishes with the Bulgars earlier in the year, and Orljak was reached on the following day.

This completed a long circular trek which, lasting three weeks, had taken the Regiment from Greece through Serbia, thence turning right-handed through Bulgaria, and eventually back into Greece once more.

By the 15th the Lothian and Border Horse, and also the Surrey Yeomanry, had joined the Regiment, thus forming a Brigade of which Lieut.-Colonel Neilson was given command, with rank of Brigadier-General, on the 30th, Captain B. H. G. Arkwright going with him as Brigade-Major. On this change being made, Major Tremayne took command of the Regiment.

Orders came on the 15th for a move to Nigrita and Neohori, near the mouth of the Struma river, and the general supposition, which proved to be right, was that this indicated an advance to the Turkish frontier and possibly beyond it.

The men were now practically in rags, and though every sort of ordnance store was urgently required none were as yet available. As frequently happened, however, just as the Regiment was about to move off on its new trek, every conceivable kind of ordnance store was flung at it. These included winter clothing, which, for lack of transport, had to be carried by the men. This delayed the move till 1 o'clock, when the Regiment at last got away after a fussing morning, and Nigrita was reached the same night—a long march. Neohori was reached next day after a twenty-four mile march, and camp was pitched near the river. All suffered from heavy attacks from mosquitoes in consequence. The march was resumed on the 18th, and Orfano was reached early in the afternoon, which allowed time for everyone to have a much-needed wash. As the villages here were derelict, all hands turned on to search for vegetables in the deserted gardens. During this march the most easterly lines of the Bulgars were passed, and these proved to be exceedingly strong. All the Greek villages passed through produced innumerable children, who all claimed Bulgar soldiers as their fathers. The frontier town of Kavalla was reached after two days' march via Provista, and was found to be already full of Greek and French troops, who had been sent there by sea. Like most Macedonian towns, Kavalla, though it looked delightful from a distance, proved to be inexpressibly dirty on nearer acquaintance. In all the towns and villages recently passed there proved to be not only a shortage of water but a great scarcity of food, in so much that the inhabitants in many cases were found to be on the verge of starvation. Kavalla was no exception, and must have suffered horribly, for its graveyards were full to overflowing, with, in many cases, the dead only partially buried.

o

IN BULGARIA AGAIN

Camp was pitched a mile east of the town, on the seashore, and everyone was able to indulge in a good and much-needed bathe. A day's rest was allowed here, but on the 22nd the march was resumed, and Sarisaban was reached. Here some vegetables were found in derelict gardens, and these formed a most welcome addition to the pot, as rations were still very short.

The Regiment was now once more in Bulgaria proper, and on the following day Kojunkoi, one-and-a-half miles east of Xanthi, was reached. In both these places squalor prevailed, and the reception to the Allied troops was far from cordial.

By this time the column had grown into an imposing force—at least if seen from a distance—as four or five days' rations had to be taken, and this entailed a train of upwards of 1,000 mules.

Melekli was reached on the 24th, and after passing through Gumuldzina, a fairly large place boasting a few shops and a number of Bulgar officers, who were swaggering about with no air of defeat, bivouac was made at Karagac on the 25th. Once more the rain descended, and continued all night, drenching everyone. By this time everybody was extremely tired from the continual marching. After two more days' marching Dedeagatch was reached, after passing through a most desolate and almost uninhabited country. Along the whole of this sector of the coast the Bulgar had dug strong and heavily-wired trenches, to guard against a landing to outflank them. It will be remembered that this town was shelled on several occasions by the Allied fleet.

Camp was pitched three miles north-east of the town, and about five from the Turkish frontier, whence it was reported that the Turks, together with a German Division, were waiting to offer resistance.

It was now twelve days since the Regiment had left Orljak, and eleven of these had been spent in long marches and in an almost continual downpour of rain. No news had been received from the outside world during this time. On the 30th the Regiment was joined by two squadrons of Lothian and Border Horse and a Brigade was now formed. As no orders to move arrived, the Regiment remained where it was except for frequent changes of camp owing to the rain and consequent mud. When rain did stop, its place was taken by a heavy cold dew at nights, which was almost as bad. Men and horses, however, got a much-needed rest, and in the first week of November some canteen stores became procurable. Dearth of news was the worst hardship, as only one mail had been received since the Regiment left Orljak. Even rumour was silent for once. Amongst other things which went to make life miserable was the shortage of firewood, even for cooking purposes ; everything burnable was eagerly sought for, and even the roots of old vine trees had to be utilised.

WELCOME NEWS

When things were looking blackest a sudden change, as is often the way, came over the scene. Someone on November 12th happened to ride into Dedeagatch for canteen stores, and came hastening back with the news of the armistice in France, and with the even more welcome announcement that the Regiment was to return to Salonica forthwith. As it turned out, this was easier to say than to do, for by now the horses and mules were almost totally without shoes, and the Regiment immobile in consequence. A cold north-east wind with rain continued for the next four days, when a consignment of shoes actually arrived. What matter that these were originally intended for heavy draft horses ? All hands were turned on to shoeing, and though the shoes, of course, did not fit in the slightest, they were induced to stay on, which was the main thing, and by the 18th the Regiment was ready and commenced its return march on the same day.

o2

It was annoying to think that by sea the return would have taken only twenty hours, whilst the march by land would take at an estimate eighteen days, but no one much cared, for all felt that their noses were at last set on the homeward track.

Each Regiment of the Brigade took it in turns to lead the way, but I find a note in the Diary to the effect that the most desirable place in the column was that immediately in rear of the Border Horse, in so much that as they dropped so many things the Regiment following was enabled to make good all deficiencies. Probably this canard is merely a social amenity !

I will not weary the reader with a description of the return march, but will content myself with stating that the weather conditions continued, if anything, even worse, for in addition to the perpetual rain, winter was rapidly coming on, and it was now much colder. Macedonia, with a hard north-east wind and sleet, is the coldest place I have yet met with. On several occasions owing to the cold the greatest difficulty in saddling up in the mornings was experienced owing to the men being half frozen.

During the march, on November 23rd to be precise, to every officer and man's deepest regret, news came through that Lieutenant H. E. Gillett had died in hospital. This officer, who had commenced the war as a Troop Sergeant, had won his commission through sheer ability. He had done splendid work with the machine-guns, was famous for his inventive faculty, and even more so for his pluck and invariable cheerfulness. He was one of the many victims of malaria, and his loss was a very real one to the Regiment, and his innumerable friends, and was felt even more keenly from the fact that it took place when hostilities were over and the return home so eagerly looked for.

On December 3rd the Regiment reached Sarigol once more, and here its history practically ends, though there were one or two short moves made subsequently.

The winter months were quite uneventful, and owing to their general unpleasantness, are best forgotten. Demobilisation, to the joy of everyone, was commenced almost immediately, though it was considerably retarded owing to an outbreak of influenza in the Regiment, which unhappily caused several deaths at practically the eleventh hour.

By the middle of April, 1919, demobilisation was complete, with the exception of the Cadre, which sailed for home early in May.

On May 22nd the Cadre, under the command of Major J. N. D'Arcy Clark, reached Derby, where, after an absence of four years and ten months, they were met by the Lord-Lieutenant of the County and the Mayor of Derby, and were accorded a civic welcome in the Market Place.

CHAPTER XIV

EXIT THE YEOMANRY

ARMOURED CARS OR ARTILLERY ?

ANY hopes that were entertained of the Derbyshire Yeomanry being retained as cavalry are now abandoned. When permission was given to raise the Regiment again after the war no definite promise was given that any of the regiments granted this favour other than the ten senior regiments would be allowed to continue permanently as cavalry. However, Derbyshire, with other units, quickly took advantage of the offer, and despite the difficulties then experienced in the matter of recruiting in some districts, the Derbyshire Yeomanry were the first to attain full strength. When this was accomplished it was hoped that if any additional units were retained Derbyshire would be one of them. The authority to continue as cavalry expires in May, 1922, but already the War Office has definitely intimated that there is no prospect of the Regiment continuing as at present constituted, and giving it the option, in the interests of economy, of immediately changing into an artillery or armoured car unit—its ultimate form.

The War Office circular points out that as the Territorial Army is to be the second line of defence, it is imperative that the proportion of artillery and certain other arms to cavalry and infantry must be far greater than that which obtained prior to the war.

The wisdom of these changes, so far as the cavalry is concerned, has been challenged in Parliament and elsewhere. Those who stand for the retention of the cavalry units argue that, whereas an infantry soldier can be created in a comparatively short space of time, it requires a much longer period to turn out an efficient horse soldier.

However, it appears too late to make any alteration so far as these units are concerned, and application has been made to form an Armoured Car Company. This alternative was considered the more suitable for several reasons. To have become artillery would have entailed clashing with other units in the districts, and another disadvantage would have been that Derbyshire would amalgamate with Nottinghamshire Yeomanry to form army troops. An armoured car company strikes a note of novelty, and should attract a type of men untouched by existing units in the district. Derby, as an engineering centre, should supply just the right sort of recruit for this arm. Another big point in favour of the armoured car is that the unit will be more or less on its own. Those who have had any experience of the army will understand the significance of this.

The Company would consist, in addition to the cars, of tenders and motor-cycles. One concession, it appears, would remain. If the application is approved, the title of the new unit will be The Derbyshire Yeomanry Armoured Car Company. Under the terms of enlistment, members of the Yeomanry will not be compelled to continue when the transformation takes place, but will, in fact, be discharged and reattested in the new unit.

HISTORY OF THE REGIMENT

The passing of the Derbyshire Yeomanry as such will occasion a feeling of deep regret in the hearts of many who have become attached to the Regiment through personal association, or who have followed its splendid history with feelings of local pride. The unit was raised 127 years ago, and there will be one source of satisfaction amid the manifestations of grief at the decision come to. The record of the Regiment in the late war, following upon the distinctions won in the South African campaign, was a fitting climax to its long and honourable history. It is particularly interesting at this epoch to recall how the Regiment was started and some of the principal events associated with it.

Following upon the secession of the American Colonies, England had just reattained its internal prosperity and foreign ascendancy when, in 1792, war broke out with France. This state of affairs led to the formation of Volunteer companies " for the better protection of the country against invasion and alarm." In the following year Mr. Pitt introduced a Bill to facilitate the raising of a Volunteer and Yeomanry force by voluntary contribution. At the Derby Easter Sessions, held on April 29th, 1794, a resolution was forwarded to the High Sheriff of the County, asking him to call a meeting for the purpose of carrying into effect the recommendations of the Government. From the files of the *Derby Mercury* we gather that a meeting was held at Derby on May 21st, when the gentlemen and yeomen of the county pledged themselves to be in readiness in support of the civil power " for the suppression of riots and tumults of all descriptions and of any case of real danger within the country." It was also agreed to raise a voluntary subscription, and that in aid of such subscription application be made to Parliament for the grant of a sum of money " levied as a fine upon the county on default of raising its militia, more than twenty years ago, which money still remains in the hands of various county officers."

The subscription list was headed by Lord G. H. Cavendish (for the Duke of Devonshire) with £500, and among other names associated with the effort were Mr. G. M. Mundy, the Hon. H. Sedley (for Lord Vernon), Mr. Richard Arkwright, Mr. Sitwell Sitwell, Mr. Hugo Meynell, Lord Scarsdale, Lord George H. Cavendish, Sir R. Burdett, Sir Henry Hunloke, Sir R. Wilmot (Chaddesden), Sir R. Wilmot (Osmaston), Mr. Hugh Bateman, Mr. Thomas Burrow, Rev. H. C. Morewood, Sir Henry Cavendish, and Lord Harrington.

FIRST APPOINTMENTS

The Derbyshire Yeomanry Cavalry was eventually raised, and the *London Gazette* of October 22nd, 1794, contained the following notice : Derbyshire Regiment of Fensible Cavalry : Lieut.-Colonel Commandant, Henry Bathurst, Esq. ; Major, Robert Cheney, Esq. ; Captains, Sitwell Sitwell, John Hayne, and Edward Miller Mundy, Esqs. ; Capt. Lieut., Sir Robert Wilmot (of Chaddesden); Lieutenants, Sir Henry Harpur, Bart., William Drury Lowe, Esq. ; Cornets, Sir Robert Wilmot (of Osmaston), Bart., Francis Mundy, Cornelius Heathcote Rhodes, and Henry H. Hunter, Esqs.

In all £7,200 was raised by subscription. The unit was first called out during the famine of 1795, when some colliers from Newhall and Swadlincote tried to obtain wheat at reduced prices by force. They went to Burton with the object of making a demonstration, but desisted. The presentation of the standard took place on October 9th, 1795, when the five troops paraded at Derby, and Lieut.-Colonel Bathurst received the standard from Lady Harrington. Afterwards the troops were marched to the Siddals and were passed in review before the Earl of Harrington ; H.R.H. the Duke D'Angoulesme, accompanied by the Earl of Moira and other officers of distinction, were also present. In the evening there was a brilliant ball, which, according to the *Mercury*, " was honoured by beauty and elegance." .

In 1797 the two troops from Derby marched to the north of the county, and joined two other troops already assembled there to support the magistrates and deputy lieutenants in carrying into execution the Supplementary Militia Act. A disturbance was prevented, and the thanks of the lieutenants and magistrates were tendered to the regiment for their valuable services.

Peace came in 1801, and after this it appears there were three denominations of irregular cavalry in the United Kingdom, Yeomanry, Volunteer Cavalry, and Provisional Cavalry. In 1803 the Volunteer Cavalry was reorganized on a more definite basis, and Sir Henry Harpur, of Calke Abbey, took the Colonelcy, a position he held to the time of his death. The following year the Regiment had its first parade of permanent duty, or as we should term it now, its first camp, and in anticipation of an inspection the C.O. issued certain orders which make interesting reading at the present day. Among them were the following : " The Quartermaster's dress to be the blue pantaloons, Hussar boots, black belt, but the chain wings of the jacket are not to have the appendage of gold fringe worn by commissioned officers and feather not longer than privates. The gentlemen to wear their hair cropped quite short, Quartermaster the same, but to wear powder on duty. Officers to wear regulation queues on public days and black silk handkerchiefs tied behind, as being tied before is considered a naval distinction. Officers should, on all field days, wear white gloves and pouch belts and knots, and, on days of ceremony or parade, white breeches, white sword, knots and belts, straight-topped military boots, silver chain spurs, etc."

" SNUFFED OUT."

The Yeomanry did good work on the occasion of the Luddite riots in 1811 until relieved by the Scots Greys. The Brandreth riots, the result of a political agitation, were chiefly " snuffed out," says Dr. Cox, by the promptness of the Derbyshire Yeomanry under the command of Major Sir Robert Wilmot.

Other minor disturbances engaged the attention of the unit, and in 1826 Lieut.-Colonel Sir Robert Wilmot was presented with a piece of massive plate of superb workmanship in grateful recognition of his zealous devotion to the interest of the corps for a period of thirty years. In June of that year the Yeomanry assembled for the last time as a Regiment, and was inspected by Lieut.-Colonel Radcliffe on Sinfin Moor. The inspecting officer declared his gratification at finding it his duty to report to H.R.H. the Commander-in-Chief his opinion that the Derbyshire Yeomanry were superior, not only in the soldier-like appearance of the men, the general equipment and the goodness of their horses, but also in their field movements and discipline, to any corps of Yeomanry which he had inspected that year.

The necessity for maintaining the Yeomanry seemed to have passed away, and a circular letter issued by the Government intimated that no allowance would be made to any Yeomanry force which had not been called out in aid of civil power for ten years. Thus, after thirty years the Regiment ceased to exist as such. The Radbourne troop continued its services gratuitously, and in 1830 was restarted with pay and allowances, and increased from fifty to ninety men. The disturbances associated with the passing of the Reform Bill in Parliament led the Government to authorise the formation of Yeomanry troops, and the Derby and Chaddesden Hussars made their first public appearance in March, 1832. The following month saw a newly-raised corps at Wirksworth, and later another independent troop appeared at Repton and Gresley. The latter troops were, by order of the Secretary of State, disbanded, but five years later the last named was raised again by Mr. Colville, M.P. The next most important event was the Chartist riot at Ashbourne in 1842. On December 1st, 1843, the Queen visited Chatsworth, and the three independent troops of Derbyshire Yeomanry did escort duty: Radbourne (Lieut. Hurt), Derby and Chaddesden (Capt. Story), and Gresley (Capt. Colville, M.P.). The Yeomanry were called out at other times, and in 1863 met for the last time as independent troops. In the following year they were formed into one regiment, with 239 officers and other ranks.

CENTENARY

The services of the Yeomanry do not seem to have been required again in the capacity which they had so often served, and they proceeded with their training, and always maintained a high state of efficiency. The centenary of the regiment was celebrated in May, 1894, by a ball held at the Midland Hotel. A distinguished company assembled, including representatives from units in the locality and neighbouring counties.

The opportunity for active service came with the outbreak of the Boer War, and the first draft numbered one hundred. They were the first contingent of Yeomanry to leave England, but, owing to the slow speed of the vessel, not the first to land in South Africa. Another draft of fifty went out, and among the officers who served then were Lieut.-Colonel Holden, Capt. Dugdale, Capt. Gisbourne, Lieut. Power, Surgeon-Capt. Wilson, and Mr. W. T. Aulton (Veterinary Officer).

The Yeomanry were in action on a number of occasions, in one of which they distinguished themselves with a company of the Grenadier Guards. General French personally thanked the O.C. of the Grenadiers and Captain Dugdale upon their conduct. One incident serves to show the spirit of the men. Lieut. Power, while in command of a patrol, was attacked by a larger force of Boers, whose commander sent a letter calling upon the patrol to surrender within fifteen minutes, after which he would not guarantee any lives or give quarter. Although just wounded and bleeding profusely, Lieut. Power wrote on the letter, " We are Englishmen, and cannot surrender." The gallant little band held out for an hour or more until relieved, and Lieut. Power received the D.S.O.

The Regiment had the honour of providing the Royal escort on the occasion of His Majesty's visit to the Royal Show, held at Derby on June 29th, 1921. This was the last mounted parade performed by the Regiment prior to their conversion to an Armoured Car Company.

LIST OF OFFICERS WHO SERVED WITH
THE REGIMENT OVERSEAS

LIEUT.-COLONELS.

Bentinck, Lord Henry.
Neilson, W.
Lance, F. F. H.
Strutt, G. A.

MAJORS.

Power, W. O.
D'Arcy Clark, J. N.
Birchenough, R. P.
Branfill, C. A.
Dudley Carleton, The Hon.
Johnson, J. G.
Shuttleworth, A. A.
Tremayne, J.
Winterbottom, G.

CAPTAINS.

Allsebrook, G. C.
Arkwright, B. H. G.
Betterton, A. H.
Brocklebank, R. H., Adjutant
   (9th Lancers).
Buckston, G. M.
Chetwynd, T.
Jackson, C. R.
Rawlinson, E. H. C.
Sir Oswald Mosley, Bart.
Sherrard, J. O.
Swanwick, F. B.
The Lord Vernon.
Wilson, R. M. (M.O.).
Wright, F. E.
Huddy, G. P. B. (M.O.).
Bonavin, V. J. (M.O.).
Power, G. (V.O.).

LIEUTENANTS.

Archer, G. O.
Blanksby, W. J.
Bowmer, T. R.
Blatch, W. D.
Burdett, A. G.
Carman, J. S.
Domleo, S. J.
Drury, G. H.
Dumat, F. A.
Feilden, R. O.
Feilden, W. M. B.
Fowke, L. H.
Gillett, H. E.
Gilpin, O. P.
Gilpin, E.
Hayward, A. S.
Hodgson, J. B. (Quartermaster).
Humphries, R. H.
Inger, A.
Keith, A. M.
Lowe, W. F.
Monk, J. R.
Montgomery, W. A.
McMaster, S.
Rogers, J.
Sadler, M. C. S.
Vaughan, E. H.
Ward, A. H.
Watkins, V. C.
Watkins, G. B.
Willan, A. R.
Wilson, S. R.
Worthington, G.
Wragg, T. A.
Wright, S. D.
Aulton, R. M. (V.O.).

SECOND-LIEUTENANT.

Howitt, C.

LIST, IN RANKS, OF THOSE KILLED OR DIED AS A RESULT OF SERVICE

23/8/15.	1961	Private Burdett, G. ..	Died from wounds.
20/8/15.	1408	Private Orme, A. ..	Killed in action.
21/8/15.	2175	Private Milnes, G. H...	,, ,,
,,	1691	Private Lowe, H. ..	,, ,,
,,	1952	Private Wingfield, S...	,, ,,
,,	1111	Sergeant Raines, S. ..	,, ,,
,,	487	Corpl. Lomas, T. ..	,, ,,
,,	1468	Lance-Cpl. Jones, A. B.	,, ,,
,,	1509	Private Whiting, E. ..	,, ,,
,,	1393	Private Kenworthy, G.	,, ,,
22/8/15.	672	Sergeant Elliot, A. ..	,, ,,
,,	1677	Private Graney, G. ..	,, ,,
25/8/15.	1906	Private Mattison, L. D.	,, ,,
23/8/15.	1793	Private Wall, J. ..	Died.
,,	1427	Lance-Cpl. Brown, J. M.	Killed in action.
28/8/15.	1205	Sergeant Bush, H. ..	Died from wounds.
21/8/15.	1602	Private Barnes, J. ..	Killed in action.
22/8/15.	1587	Lance-Cpl. Kirk, G. W.	,, ,,
,,	146	Private Gregory, W. ..	,, ,,
13/9/15.	1743	Private Worth, H. ..	Died.
5/9/15.	1933	Private Howard, W. ..	,,
23/9/15.	1955	Private Fletcher, F. ..	
8/9/15.	1048	Private Robinson, T. P.	Died from wounds.
6/9/15.	1811	Lance-Cpl. Holden, J. W.	Killed in action.
5/9/15.	1979	Private Pakes, S. ..	Died from wounds.
22/8/15.	1789	Private Norris, H. G...	Killed in action.
22/8/15.	1275	Squadron - Q. M. S. Wright, W. ..	Died from wounds.
		Captain Lord Vernon..	Died.
6/10/15.	2037	Lance-Cpl. Canty, E. ...	
22/8/15.	1711	Private Copeland, A. A.	Killed in action.
,,	2021	Private Poyser, A. ..	,, ,,
28/9/15.	1036	Corporal Brookes, F. ...	Died from wounds.
12/9/15.	1752	Private Endsor, G. ..	Killed in action.
20/11/15.	2331	Private Coulton, E. H.	Died.
22/8/15.	1500	Lance-Cpl. Lee, W. R.	Killed in action.
,,	2165	Private Bryan, M. ..	,, ,,
21/8/15.	1570	Private Bayley, G. ..	,, ,,
,,	1668	Private Moss, E. ..	,, ,,
11/2/16.	1488	Sergeant Martin, N. A.	Died.

18/8/16.	1763	Private Mills, F. ..	Killed in action.
20/8/16.	1496	Lance-Cpl. Wright, L.	Died when prisoner of war.
,,	2040	Corporal Weston, T. ..	Killed in action.
,,	2055	Private Boddice, W.	,, ,,
,,	1520	Private Hall, H. H. ..	,, ,,
,,	1575	Private Holt, O. A. ..	,, ,,
,,	1954	Private Mansfield, P. ..	Died from wounds as prisoner of war.
,,	1900	Private Austin, A. ..	Killed in action.
,,	1149	Private Hall, P. W. ..	,, ,,
8/9/16.	2093	Cpl. Whitehouse, L. V.	Died.
18/10/16.	2099	Lance-Cpl. Auckland ..	Died when prisoner of war.
6/12/16.	2592	Private Freeman, J. F.	Died from wounds.
27/12/16.	2401	Private Ray, W. G. ..	Died.
22/1/17.	1900	Corpl. Wood, E. ..	Died from wounds.
10/6/17.	75162	Private Hassal, P. ..	,, ,,
19/6/17.	75342	Private Connor, J. ..	,, ,,
23/6/17.	75653	Private Labon, W. ..	Killed in action.
25/6/17.	75976	Private Thornby, J. A.	,, ,,
1/7/17.	75396	Corpl. Hanson, A. ..	Killed in action.
9/8/17.		Major Winterbottom, Guy	,, ,,
10/9/17.	76140	Private Buck, A. ..	Died.
30/1/18.	75023	Staff-Sgt.-Maj. Buman, F.	,,
18/2/18.	73687	Private Smith, D. ,.	,,
13/3/18.	75965	Private Martin, R. H.	Died from wounds.
12/6/18.	76149	Private Denby, H. G...	Killed in action.
8/7/18.	76067	Private Cowmeadow, V. H.	Died.
		R.S.M. Simpson ..	,,
20/9/18.	76174	Staff-Sergt. Milligan, J.	,,
3/10/18.	75085	Private Garrett, F. W.	,, ,,
19/11/18.	75841	Private Inger, A. J. ..	,,
21/11/18.	75125	Private Litchfield, G...	,,
23/11/18.		Lieut. Gillett, H. E.	,,
5/11/18.	75669	Private Wilbraham, L.	,,
26/11/18.	76198	Private Storey, A. ..	,,
29/11/18.	75792	Private Benyon, J. C...	,,
4/1/19.	D15725	Private Middleton, J...	,,
20/1/19.	75747	Private Fireday, S. P.	,,
1/1/19.	75584	Private Wheway, H. ..	,,
24/3/19.	75805	Private Hallam, F. ..	,,
23/3/19.	95967	Private Howard, N. ..	,,

LIST OF HONOURS

Lieut.-Colonel Neilson—Mentioned twice, Salonica; Brevet Lieut.-Colonel; Distinguished Service Order; Order of Kara George with Swords.

Lieut.-Colonel Strutt—Mentioned Gallipoli and France.

Major Lance—Mentioned Gallipoli.

Major D'Arcy Clark—Mentioned Salonica.

Major Branfill—Mentioned Salonica; Military Cross; Order of Redeemer, 4th Class (Greek).

Major Johnson—Mentioned Salonica; Distinguished Service Order.

Major Winterbottom—Mentioned Gallipoli; Order of White Eagle (4th Class).

Captain Chetwynd—Mentioned Gallipoli; Military Cross.

Captain Jackson—Mentioned Salonica; Military Cross.

Lieut. Blanksby—Mentioned Salonica; Military Cross; Croix de Guerre.

Lieut. Bowmer—Mentioned Salonica.

Lieut. Domleo—Croix de Guerre, with Palms; Military Cross.

Lieut. Feilden, W. M. B.—Mentioned Gallipoli; Military Cross; Italian Medal (Silver).

Lieut. Lowe—Mentioned Salonica; Military Cross.

Lieut. Saddler—Military Cross.

Lieut. Vaughan—Mentioned Salonica; Military Cross.

Staff-Sergt.-Major Heath—Mentioned Salonica; Distinguished Conduct Medal.

Staff-Sergeant Robinson—Mentioned Salonica.

Staff-Sergeant Thomas—Military Medal.

Sergeant Abbott—Mentioned Salonica; Italian Bronze Medal.

Sergeant Cuff—Military Medal.

Sergeant Gillott—Mentioned Gallipoli and Salonica; Military Medal.

Sergeant Goodall, L. L.—Mentioned Salonica.

Sergeant Mansfield—Mentioned Salonica; Military Medal; Distinguished Conduct Medal.

Sergeant Mason—Mentioned Salonica.

Sergeant Outram—Military Medal.

Sergeant Pratt—Military Medal.

Sergeant Tarrey—Cross of Kara George.
Sergeant Sutton—Medaille Barbatie, 2nd Class (Roumanian).
Sergeant Wright, J. H. D.—Mentioned Salonica ; Military Medal.
Corporal Atkin—Mentioned Salonica.
Corporal Limbert—Mentioned Salonica.
Corporal Pratt—Mentioned Salonica.
Corporal Snaith—Military Medal.

Lance-Corporal Ainsworth—Mentioned Salonica.
Lance-Corporal Bibby—Mentioned Gallipoli.
Lance-Corporal Blount, W.—Mentioned Gallipoli.

Private Aldridge—Military Medal.
Private Bonnett—Mentioned Salonica ; Serbian Gold Medal.
Private Gambles—Meritorious Service Medal.
Private Glaves—Mentioned Gallipoli.
Private Hallam—Mentioned Salonica.
Private Jones, V. S.—Military Medal.
Private Mansfield—Military Medal.

A LIST OF "MENTIONED IN DESPATCHES"

Major Lance, F. FitzHugh   ..
Lieut.-Colonel Strutt, G. H.*..
Captain Winterbottom, G.   ..
Lieut. Chetwynd, A. H. T.   ..
Lieut. Feilden, W. M. B.   ..
1395 Sergeant Gillott, H.   ..
1755 Lance-Corpl. Bibby, J. ..
1559 Lance-Corpl. Blount, W...
655 Private Glaves, D.   ..
Captain Johnson, J. G.   ..
1588 Corpl. Abbott, W.   ..
2118 Private Bonnell, T.   ..
Lieut. Jackson, G. R. ..   ..
Second-Lieut. Lowe, W. F.   ..
Lieut.-Colonel Neilson, W.
Major D'Arcy Clark, J. N.   ..
Major Johnson, J. G., D.S.O.
Captain Branfill, C. A.   ..
Lieut. Vaughan, E. H.   ..
Second-Lieut. Blanksby, W. J.
Second-Lieut. Bowmer, T. R.
5053 Sergeant Gillott, H. J...
75493 Sergeant Goodall, L. L.
75079 S.S.M. Heath ..   ..
75041 Sergeant Mansfield, C. H.
75576 Corporal Pratt, F.   ..
75131 S.S. Robinson, H.
75031 Sergt. Wright, J. H. D. V.
75127 Sergeant Muson, P. N.
75394 Private Hallam, B.   ..
Major and Brevet Lieut.-Colonel
(Temp. Lieut.-Colonel) Neilson
W. (4th Hussars).
75753 Lance-Cpl. (Acting Cpl.)
Ainsworth, W.
75166 Corporal Atkin, W.   ..
75136 Corporal (Acting Sergt.)
Limbert, T.

Sir Ian Hamilton's, 11/12/15.
*Also Sir Douglas Haig's,
France, August, 1919.

Sir Charles Munro's, 13/7/16.

Lieut.-Gen. Milne's, 8/10/16.

Lieut.-Gen. Milne's, 29/3/17.

Lieut.-Gen. Milne's, 25/10/17.

Lieut.-Gen. Milne's, 25/10/17.

Lieut.-Gen. Milne's, 1918.

Lieut.-Gen. Milne's, 1919.

HONOURS WON BY MEMBERS OF THE UNIT FOR SERVICE IN THE FIELD

"IMMEDIATE AWARDS"

75124 Sergeant Outram, J. W.   Military Medal, 6/4/18.

75041 Sergeant Mansfield, C. H.
75574 Sergeant Pratt, F. ..
75779 Private Mansfield, J. ..
75871 Private Jones, V. S. .. } Military Medal, 1/10/17.
75053 Sergeant Gillott, H. J.
75031 Sergeant Wright, J. H. D.

Captain Chetwynd, A. H. T. ..
Lieut. Feilden, W. M. B. .. } Military Cross, 13/7/16.

Major Winterbottom, Guy .. White Eagle (4th Class), 27/10/16.

2118 Private Bonnell, T. .. Gold Medal (Serbian).
1574 Corporal Snaith, G. F. .. Military Medal, 21/12/16.
Major Johnson, J. G. .. .. D.S.O., 1/1/17.
Lieut. Feilden, W. M. B. .. Silver Medal (Italian).
1588 Sergeant Abbott, W. .. Bronze Medal (Italian).
75279 Sergeant Cuff, F. .. Military Medal, 30/3/17.
75106 Corporal Dungworth ..
—— Private Walker .. } Military Medal, 26/6/17.
Lieut. Lowe, W. F. .. .. Military Cross, 19/11/17.
75694 Private Aldridge, A. G... Military Medal, 2/11/17.
Major (Temp. Lieut.-Col.) Neilson, W. (4th Hussars) .. Brevet Lieut.-Colonel.
Major Branfill, C. A. ..
Captain Jackson, G. R. .. } Military Cross, 1/1/18.
Lieut. Vaughan, E. H.

75041 Sergeant Mansfield, C. H. } D.C.M., 1/1/18.
75079 Staff-Sgt.-Maj. Heath, H.
75733 Staff-Sgt. Thomas, J. H. Military Medal, 1/12/17.
Brevet Lieut.-Col. Neilson, W... The Order of Kara George with Swords, 5/2/18.

76044 Sergeant Tarrey, F. .. Cross of Kara George, 5/2/18.
Lieut. Blanksby, W. .. ..
Lieut. Domleo, S. J. .. .. } Military Cross, 19/10/18.
Major Branfill, C. A. .. Order of Redeemer, 4th Class (Greek).

Lieut. Saddler, M. C. .. .. Military Cross, 1/1/19.
Lieut. Domleo, S. J. .. .. Croix de Guerre with Palms, 16/1/19.

Brig.-General Neilson, W. .. D.S.O., 1/1/19.
76818 Private Gambles, G. W. Meritorious Service Medal, 5/6/18.

75252 Sergeant Sutton, C. .. Medaille Barbatie, Sis Gadinba, 2nd Class (Roumanian), 11/3/19.

www.ingramcontent.com/pod-product-compliance
Lightning Source LLC
Chambersburg PA
CBHW030934150426
42812CB00064B/2852/J